Champagne Memories
..and how
Brian Clough
changed my life

Part of the proceeds of this book will go to the Royal British Legion, a charity that continues to play a large part in Colin's life, and the NSPCC, a cause that was close to the hearts of Brian and Barbara Clough. The non-profit tribute website, brianclough. com, will also benefit.

First published 2014 by DB Publishing, an imprint of JMD Media Ltd, Nottingham, United Kingdom.

ISBN 9781780910444

Champagne Memories

..and how

Brian Clough

changed my life

My Story – Colin Shields with Marcus Alton

DB PUBLISHING

Marcus Alton was still at school when he began writing a regular sports column in the local parish magazine, securing an exclusive interview with the new chairman of Nottingham Forest FC who lived in the same village.

He then joined the Newark Advertiser newspaper, winning the title of Midlands Sports Journalist of the Year. He has worked for the BBC for more than 25 years and is a senior journalist.

In August 2000, Marcus set-up the nonprofit-making website, brianclough. com. Marcus has written two previous books about Brian: 'Young Man, You've Made My Day,' and 'The Day I Met Brian Clough' which includes memories from his family, friends and fans

Contents

Dedicated to my daughter, Susan,
who we miss so much.

Introduction

"Enjoy it while you can, it won't be here forever." Those few words to me from Brian as we travelled to a match in the car will stay with me for many years. I enjoyed some wonderful times with him and I can now look back on those experiences and share them.

In the early days of our friendship, he would say, "Call me Brian." But I daren't call him Brian – I was so in awe of him. Then, as time went by, I felt relaxed in his company and I was able to talk to him easily as a friend. Eventually it felt the most natural thing in the world to call him Brian.

Many of my really close friends, including Brian, have now passed away and I'm left with the memories. But recalling them has been thoroughly enjoyable and has put a spark back in my life. Over the years, I've not made a habit of talking about my memories of Brian – many of the stories I've recalled here are being shared for the first time.

It's been a wonderful experience working on this book with Marcus Alton, without whose help it would not have been possible. His experience, knowledge and good humour have been invaluable throughout the whole process. I'm pleased to say we have shared some laughs along the way, as well as remembering some particularly poignant moments. The many conversations included in this book have been recounted as accurately as possible. I would also like to thank my friends Jim and Jill Lowe for intro-ducing me to Marcus in the first place. A mention, too, for my friend and photographer Charlie Noble.

To look back and recall the wonderful times I shared with Brian has re-kindled memories which are very special to me. While my close friendship with the most charismatic manager football has ever known was not always plain sailing (I've been on the wrong end of a telling-off a number of times!), I would not have swapped it for the world.

Brian was kind, thoughtful and loyal. We trusted each other implicitly, to the extent that he once paid me a huge compliment by saying that if he could have chosen an extra brother, it would have been me.

As a fan who closely followed Brian's achievements at both Derby County and Nottingham Forest, being part of the 'Bring Back Clough' campaign at Derby and being allowed to travel on the team coach at Forest, I have friends at both ends of the A52, or Brian Clough Way. And for that I would like to thank them all.

Without many of those friends, this story would have been extremely difficult to tell. But of course, without Brian it would have been impossible. Having originally watched Brian's teams from the terraces, I could never have dreamed that he would eventually let me travel on the players' coach on a regular basis (hallowed ground as far as Brian was concerned!), that we would drive in the car together to matches and social events, enjoy holidays in the sunshine and that I would rub shoulders with other big names in football management, including Sir Bobby Robson.

Looking back, I still consider myself very lucky to have become such a close friend of a man I regarded as a hero – and still do. I never took my friendship with Brian – or the opportunities he gave me – for granted. This book, I hope, will illustrate that – and the great debt I owe him for the fantastic times we shared.

Now then, young man...

It has been an absolute privilege and pleasure to get to know Colin and listen to his memories of life with Brian Clough. As a big Clough fan for many years, I was fascinated to hear Colin's tales of the times they spent together – in particular those occasions away from the public spotlight.

In many ways, this book will show a quality of Cloughie that many may be unfamiliar with: his love of the simple things in life, like a game of dominoes during his regular visits to the local branch of the Royal British Legion. And he was just as competitive over a game of dominoes or cards as he was in a crucial football match.

There are a few people I would like to thank for their help. A mention must go to Colin's wife, Irene, who kept me fed and watered during the many long hours Colin and I spent talking about our hero. I would also like to thank my wife, Sarah, for her encouragement and support throughout the whole process of working on the book. She has been a rock when I needed it most. Thanks, too, to my boss at the BBC, Mike Bettison, for his help in allowing me to complete this project, although I must add that it has all been carried out in my spare time! To Jill and Jim for introducing me to Colin – thank you very much. A mention must also go to Andy Ellis, for his help with some of the Derby County information. On the subject of club statistics, Colin's collection of match programmes from over the years was invaluable too. And last, but by no means least, thanks to my Mum and Dad, who encouraged my writing career at an early age. I was writing about Brian Clough when I was at primary school. More than thirty years later and he is still the focus of my work!

This book spans Colin's life, from his childhood memories supporting his local football team, to the arrival of a certain manager and the relationship, which eventually developed. I hope it will be seen as a celebration of a valued friendship between two people – one a very famous football manager; the other, a man unknown to the wider public, until now.

Marcus Alton
youngman@brianclough.com

About Marcus Alton

Marcus Alton is a BBC radio journalist and joined the corporation in December 1988. He began his career as a sports and news reporter on the *Newark Advertiser* newspaper, where he was named Midlands Sports Reporter of the Year (weekly newspapers). Marcus met Brian Clough a number of times, both as a journalist and a fan, and conducted several interviews with him. In 2005 he was part of the BBC team which won silver in the Frank Gillard Awards for its reporting of the death of Brian Clough and his memorial service. Marcus is the editor of the non-profit making website, brianclough.com, which he launched in August 2000. The website has the backing of the Clough family. He also set-up the committee that raised the money for the superb bronze statue of Brian in Nottingham city centre. Through hours of hard work and lots of fund-raising ideas, the committee smashed through its target in just 18 months, raising £70,000. Around 5,000 people gathered in the Old Market Square to watch Barbara Clough unveil the statue in November 2008. Marcus also organised the petition calling for a knighthood for Brian, which received support from thousands of fans and many well-known names. Accompanied by his wife, Sarah, and the MP Bob Laxton, he delivered the signatures and messages to 10 Downing Street. Marcus has written two previous books about Brian: *'Young Man, You've Made My Day,'* including the full story behind the website, statue and knighthood campaign; and *'The Day I Met Brian Clough'* which includes memories from his family, friends and fans.

1.

When The Ball Burst

The first time I watched Brian Clough in action for Middlesbrough, at the height of his goal-scoring exploits, I could never have imagined the dramatic effect he would have on my life – the close friendship we would share in later years and the incredible experience of watching a football genius at work.

I still feel privileged to know I was among the few people, besides the players, who Brian would allow to travel on the team coach when he was manager. Even the directors were banned! There were also times when we would travel in the car and have a good chat together – putting the world to rights.

And away from the world of football, even the mundane became memorable – on holiday in Majorca we would laugh as we carried big bags of laundry together down the side streets and across the seafront, before finding a quiet spot to relax, away from the crowds. He would give me advice about management and how I should deal with the factory staff, who I employed in the food industry. But he didn't quite grasp the fact that I couldn't simply sack someone on the spot without very good reason! Life was never dull with Brian around. We had some wonderful times. They are fantastic memories I will always treasure.

I shared some of the highs and lows of his incredible career and will never forget his immense kindness. Yes, he could be unpredictable too, that was part of his magic. You never quite knew what he was going to do or say next. And I've been on the receiving end of a telling off! But he also knew how to build you up, make you feel good about yourself. I'm only a small chap, five-feet three inches in height, but sometimes he made me feel ten feet tall. I could understand how his man management got the very best out of his players.

Brian opened the door to a whole new world for me. I met some of the biggest names in football and got to know them. Can you imagine not only meeting the great Bill Shankly, but then Brian saying: "Col, I'd like you to look after Bill today, make sure he gets anything he'd like." It was like a dream. I felt like a football millionaire. But it was all very different from another time in my life, years before, when I stood on the terraces and first saw Brian play for Middlesbrough in the 1950s.

As a centre-forward, Brian always seemed to be in the right place at the right time. I was always impressed with how he could get himself into a goal-scoring position – and usually he would score. In fact, he did that 197 times in just 213 league appearances for Middlesbrough, his hometown club. It's already widely known just how proud he was of his goal-scoring achievements at Middlesbrough and then Sunderland. In later years, he would never let anyone forget that he scored the fastest 250 goals by any player in the game. Although he was predominantly right-footed, he could score with his head and his left foot too. I watched from behind the goal at Derby County's Baseball Ground and saw him play for Middlesbrough in a few games there. Two of his goals came in a 3–0 win over Derby in April 1959 – just a few days after he had got married. He even played on his wedding day, 4 April, against Leyton Orient and, of course, he scored! Early the following year, he netted another brace against Derby, this time at Ayresome Park. I think he scored them in the last few minutes. Just like the teams that he would manage in later life, he was determined to play until that final whistle.

In those days, I was in my twenties and watching the matches as a

Derby fan, so those defeats did not go down too well with me at the time. But I could not fail to be impressed with the skill of that young centre-forward called Clough. Ever since I was a young boy, my whole life has revolved around football. As a youngster, growing up in the Derbyshire town of Alfreton, we used to play football in a school playground. But we didn't have a leather football – we couldn't afford one – so we used a tennis ball instead. And we could perform amazing tricks with that tennis ball, making it bend this way and that, as we passed it around the playground. I was in and out of different football teams but I remember playing alongside a lad called Barry Jepson, who went on to play for Peterborough, as did his brother Keith. I enjoyed our games, kicking the tennis ball around. It suited my physique, rather than using a big leather ball, as I was only slightly built – there wasn't much weight on me! I suppose it also helped develop the skills of controlling the ball, which paid dividends when we eventually played with the real thing. That opportunity came one Christmas, thanks to a surprise from my Mum, Renee.

My eyes were as big as saucers on the Christmas morning I received my first leather football. Mum had spotted it in a shop in the town and had been secretly putting money aside with the shopkeeper each week so she could buy it as a Christmas present for me. That football changed my life completely – and the lives of my friends. At last we could play proper matches with an authentic leather football, which had laces and a bladder. It increased my popularity by one hundred percent. Yes, everyone wanted a game of football with Colin! We started playing on grass and sometimes got chased off farmers' fields.

The first person I told about the football was my friend, Barry Robinson, who was a couple of years older than me. I suppose you could describe him as my mentor – he taught me how to play football and cricket. He was absolutely brilliant, a great sportsman. It was Barry who took me to see Derby County matches for the first time, when I was about 15. Up until then, I had relied on newspapers and the radio to keep me in touch with my beloved Rams.

The day Derby were at Wembley for the 1946 FA Cup Final was obviously a special one. I was only 13 and a group of us were playing football on the local recreation ground. We were all keen to find out how Derby were getting on. So we finished our game and hurried up the hill to get home. As we passed a house, we could hear the sound of a radio with commentary of the match – it was like a magnet to us. A small group of us stood outside, trying to hear what was happening. The couple who lived there saw us and said we could stay and listen to it, so we huddled around the radio on the front doorstep. We were so excited to hear the game - our team playing at Wembley. It felt such a privilege to be able to listen to it. Of course, we were told we had to behave – but we would have done anything to hear the match.

It was an incredibly exciting final – even though we could not be among the thousands of people who were at Wembley. Derby took the lead with just a few minutes remaining, thanks to an own goal. But then Charlton equalised from a free-kick. We thought Jack Stamps had won the cup for Derby when his shot beat the Charlton 'keeper – but at that moment the ball burst on its way to goal and they had to replace it! If you had written that as a script for a film, you would never have believed it. So the match went into extra-time and Derby did us proud, winning 4–1.

We were absolutely elated when Derby lifted the cup on that wonderful April day. We went home celebrating as if we, personally, had won that special trophy. The times were austere and we had not got a lot to boast about. But football was very important to the whole town – and winning the cup gave the entire community a huge lift. Things got even better when the cup went on display at our local cinema, the Empire in Alfreton. We would usually go to the pictures to watch Laurel and Hardy or Gene Autrey films – but the day that the FA Cup came to visit was an absolute showstopper. I remember walking into the room – and there it was, brightly lit and shining. At first I just stood and stared. My whole attention was focussed on that magnificent trophy, which I had only seen previously in photographs. We were then given the chance to touch it – and I don't think I washed my hands for a week afterwards! The picture of that wonderful gleaming cup is still imprinted on my memory. I have never seen it in person since, but I am lucky to say – thanks to Brian Clough – it is not the only prestigious football trophy I have been able to touch (even though it is the one that eluded him during his career).

Unfortunately for my Dad, the 1946 FA Cup victory left a very sour taste. He had been to every cup match during that season's campaign, but he could not get a ticket for the Final. All the matches were played over two legs and he hadn't missed one of them. He saw two 6–0 victories, against Luton Town in the first round and Brighton in the third round, plus all the other games. I remember him talking about the semi-final against Birmingham City, with the two legs played on a neutral ground. The first leg at Hillsborough ended in a 1–1 draw, which set-up the second leg nicely. Dad was among the 80,000 people who crammed into Maine Road, Manchester, to see Derby win the second match 4–0. As you can imagine, he was looking forward to seeing the final, but no matter how he tried he just could not get a ticket for Wembley. He was so disappointed that he vowed never to watch Derby again.

It was around that time that the relationship between by parents had also begun to turn sour. Things started to go wrong for them during the war years. My Dad had been in the Territorial Army so he was among the first to be called-up. We had moved to live in Derby before the war and my Dad worked at the chemical company British Celanese in Spondon, before becoming a store-man at the aero-engine makers Rolls Royce. He felt he had done well to move us away from the Derbyshire coal mines and find a home in the city instead. But when he came out of the Army, he was distraught to find that my Mum had moved us to Alfreton, where her own mother lived. My Dad was upset because he felt the family had simply given-up the house in Derby that he had striven so hard to secure. To be fair to my Mum, the house on Marlborough Road in the city was right next to the Rolls Royce factory – a key target for the German bombers – and she felt it just wasn't safe for me or my younger brother Trevor, who was born there in 1939. We spent night after night in the air raid shelters. Yet even in Alfreton, fourteen miles further north, we still could not escape the bombing.

One evening we were walking home from my grandmother's house, with Trevor in the pushchair, when suddenly there was the sound of aircraft and a load of incendiary bombs landed around us. I will never forget watching them explode and burst into flames. I even felt a hot spark on the back of my neck. Although the three of us survived, a number of people were killed by the bombings in the town that night. Ironically, my Mum knew all about bombs – she worked at the Raleigh cycle factory in Nottingham, which had been turned into a munitions depot. She made the striking pins that went into the British bombs. Apart from that rare occasion when we were walking home, the only times I would see my Mum was when she had finished the night shift and was getting off the bus as I was going to school.

My Grandma was looking after us most of the time because of my Mum's working hours. Each morning, as I set off for school, Mum would have a little present for me – a sweet or an apple she had been given because she was an essential war worker. It was still a close-knit family and we all looked out for each other. I had uncles and aunties who were like brothers and sisters to me. My youngest uncle was only a year older than I was. But shortly after the war, Mum and Dad got divorced. I was only about 14 and – although I probably did not realise it at the time – it must have had a big effect on me. Things were never the same again for our family. In later years it made me determined that my children should never go through the trauma of divorce. I wanted to ensure they were brought-up in a loving environment, a loving home.

I still kept in touch with Dad and, after a few years, tried to persuade him to return to watching Derby County. But he would not listen to me. I had started to watch the Rams who were by now managed by Harry Storer, celebrating the achievement of becoming Division Three North Champions in 1957. The Rams goalkeeper Terry Adlington worked with me at Blackwell Colliery – he was employed in the same electricians' work-shop – and would arrange for me to pick-up match tickets at the players' entrance at the ground. It was during those years that I saw Brian playing against us for Middlesbrough, both home and away, and I could not help but be impressed with his goal-scoring prowess. In one match, in October 1957, he put Boro 1–0 up against us after about three minutes. The final score was 3–0. As I have mentioned, it was the same score-line in April 1959 and then again in January 1960, with Brian finding the back of the net twice in each match. Although this wasn't much comfort for a Derby fan, the signing of one particular player was to change all that.

Following Harry Storer's departure in 1962 came Tim Ward and the arrival of a player who became my idol. Kevin Hector had scored 113 league goals in 176 games for Bradford when Ward surprised fans by signing him for £38,000. Derby were not used to spending that kind of money, but Hector was an instant success and became our very own goal machine. He scored on his home debut against Huddersfield Town in September 1966. Not only did Derby win 4–3 but it was a superb performance by Hector who showed he had the speed, skill and shooting power that fans like me had longed to see. Now, I'm a married man – but I don't mind telling you that I had a poster of Kevin Hector on my bedroom wall! I still treasure a photo of the time I made a presentation to him on behalf of the supporters club.

I continued my efforts to persuade my Dad to return to the Baseball Ground.

"You've got to come down and see this young lad Kevin Hector – he's something special," I told him.

Dad would reply sharply: "No, I'm not bothered about watching Derby ever again, no way." A few days later I gave it one last try: "Please come back and watch them – I can promise that you won't regret it."

Eventually, he agreed to join me at a match and from that day he never missed another game until he died. For the away matches, we would have a car full of people and my Dad would bring a basket of homing pigeons with him, which he would put in the back. We would get so far into the journey – Rotherham, for example – and then he would let the pigeons go and we would continue our way to the game. His new wife Lily would have to be at home to make a note of the time they arrived back!

With the great Alan Durban in the side too (he scored a hat-trick in that game against Huddersfield) you could sense that Derby were starting to go places. There was a feeling of excitement back on the terraces, but unfortunately the 1966–67 season fizzled out with a 17th placed finish and Tim Ward left the club. As one chapter closed, a whole new story was about to unfold and I was to meet the man who eventually changed my life.

2.

My Deal With Brian

"Who's this lad, Brian Clough?" my friends asked me when he joined Derby County in June 1967.

"Don't you remember him?" I replied. "He's the one that scored all those goals against us for Middlesbrough. What a player!"

Some of them were still not convinced. Yes, he had been able to keep Hartlepool in the Football League in his first management role (no mean feat, he would tell me in later years), but what could he do for Derby?

Brian set about transforming the club. And with his assistant Peter Taylor beside him, nothing seemed impossible for them. John O'Hare, then aged just 19, joined from Sunderland, where Brian had been impressed with the striker while coaching the youth team. The focus was on establishing a solid spine to the side – so Tranmere's Roy McFarland was snatched from under the noses of Liverpool and Everton and became one of the country's best ever centre-halves. Add John McGovern, who worked hard in the midfield engine room, and Alan Hinton, who could cross the ball with pinpoint accuracy, and the team was beginning to show signs of becoming the perfect blend.

There was just one fly in the ointment. The new manager's declaration that Derby would finish higher in the league than the previous season didn't come true. It is one of the very few Clough predictions I've known over the years that didn't become reality. Usually, when he said something, it was written in the stars and you knew it would happen. For example, take Nottingham Forest's first European Cup tie against Liverpool. Many outsiders thought Liverpool, as defending champions, would get the better of Forest. But having already beaten them in the League Cup Final and drawn two league games, the Forest players were given a psychological boost when Brian told them that Liverpool wouldn't fancy facing them again. His players went out and proved him right. Nevertheless, in that first season at Derby, Brian's talent for fortune-telling wasn't as sharp as it would be in the future – and we saw the team finish 18th, one place lower than in the previous season under Tim Ward.

The disappointing finish did not dampen the optimism of the Derby faithful. In fact during the summer of 1968 the club sold a huge number of season tickets. I'd been on a family holiday to the Isle of Wight and had just come back on the ferry when a friend asked if I'd renewed my season ticket. I said I hadn't. He then told me they had sold out.

"Don't worry," I replied, "they'll still have mine because I had it last year."

When I got back to Derby I went to the ticket office and they confirmed they had sold my season ticket – and that of my mate Sam who sat with me. I was absolutely livid. I spoke to Michael Dunford who was in charge of the office and told him exactly what I thought.

"I've been watching Derby for years and now everyone's jumping on the bandwagon and wanting to buy tickets – and you've sold my seat!" I told him.

"Oh, everyone's a Derby fan now," was the response.

I replied: "Well, I've been watching them since Harry Storer was manager. It's not a bandwagon with me."

As I was venting my frustration, Brian Clough walked in and heard the conversation. "Can I help you, Sir?" asked Brian. I explained what had happened and Brian arranged for me to have a look at where some remaining seats were available in the ground and to try them out.

"Once you've decided which seats you'd like, come back to me," said Brian. So I had a look at the various seats – I wasn't particularly happy, but I chose a couple and went back into the office.

"Have you chosen where you'd like to sit?" he asked.

I said I had, but that I didn't think my mate, who would sit with me, would be very happy about it.

"Well, this is my guarantee to you," added Brian. "Next season, when we all start again, you can have first choice of any seat you want."

That sealed it for me. Having felt very despondent that my seats had gone, I left the ticket office that day absolutely elated. And to be fair to Brian, he kept his promise. The following season I got my original seats back. It's not something you'd see very often these days – football club managers walking around a ground and speaking to fans so openly. But if you went to the ticket office at the Baseball Ground, Brian would often be there and was happy to talk to you and answer questions. It gave you such a lift because he made you feel involved and valued as a supporter. Years before, I had seen Harry Storer walking around and carrying his little dog, but he wasn't as approachable as Brian.

The special connection that Brian was to develop with the fans was clear to see when he came to speak to my branch of the Supporters Club – in Nottingham. Despite the huge rivalry with Nottingham Forest, I had become the chairman of the Nottingham branch of the Derby County Supporters Club, after moving from Blackwell Colliery to the new pit at Cotgrave in Nottinghamshire. I got on extremely well with the branch's founding member and driving force, Ron Stevenson, who remains a friend to this day. I was one of the first applicants to get a job at Cotgrave pit, working three shift patterns, including some Saturday afternoons and therefore missing a few matches. But the event I certainly didn't want to miss was the night that the Derby County manager came to speak to members of our supporters branch in Nottingham.

We used to hold our branch meetings at the Dog and Bear pub in Nottingham city centre, where the landlord, Bill Bowman, was a Derby fan and gave us the use of an upstairs room free of charge. Obviously, as we were holding a meeting of Derby fans right in the centre of Nottingham, we tried to be discreet – we didn't want the windows smashed in. Ron had originally asked Peter Taylor to come to talk to us and, on the night of the event, we all sat there expectantly. Then we heard footsteps coming up the stairs. Not only was it Peter, but Brian as well, along with his friend Michael Keeling.

It was a tremendous night and Brian said it was brilliant to have a supporters branch in Nottingham. He thought it was great to have this loyal enclave of fans in the 'enemy camp.' There was some heckling from a group of youngsters outside the pub when Brian and Peter arrived and the heckling continued during part of the meeting.

Peter turned to Brian and said: "Listen to them out there – we could soon have them eating out of our hands, couldn't we?"

They were clearly so full of confidence that a little bit of stick from rival fans only served to give them a further boost. Of course, in future years, the pair did serve up some very tasty fayre for those Forest supporters. But that night, in the upstairs room of the pub, we were completely mesmerised by our special visitors.

Brian had simply breezed into the room and the aura around him was incredible. He seemed to enjoy the question-and-answer session we held. I asked him if the players were ever allowed to have a drink before a match (I'd heard that they sometimes enjoyed a little tipple before a game).

He joked: "If they get me a goal, they can have half a bottle of whisky!"

I also asked him whether he could get hold of FA Cup Final tickets. I don't think he was impressed with the question. I didn't realise it then but everyone asked him for FA Cup Final tickets. It seemed important to me at the time because my Dad had missed out on the opportunity to go to the 1946 final. Fortunately I was able to get tickets for the 1968 Final between Everton and West Brom. But little did I know that in later years I would enjoy many Wembley trips thanks to Brian, and often looked after his young sons during those special occasions – but more of that later.

Brian and Peter's visit to our supporters club meeting in Nottingham was hailed a huge success, but it wasn't the only successful evening we had with a special guest or two. For another event we invited the midfielder Willie Carlin to come and talk to us. We received a positive reply, but were told that he needed picking-up and driving over to the meeting. So I volunteered and drove over to the Derbyshire town of Melbourne and brought Willie and his wife, Marie, into Nottingham. I got on very well with Willie, who had a reputation for getting 'stuck-in' like a little terrier on the football field. We established a good rapport with each other straightaway and he has remained a very good friend ever since. He also helped me when I ran my own company in later years.

The whole city felt alive because of the great football being played at the Baseball Ground. On the pitch, at the heart of it all, making things tick, was the legendary Dave Mackay whom Brian had persuaded to sign for Derby, in another managerial masterstroke. Mackay had been ready to leave Spurs to become assistant manager of the Scottish side, Hearts. But Brian had other plans. Mackay was turned into a sweeper at Derby and brought a fantastic swagger to the team. He was certainly tough in the tackle and the fans loved it. But he also had great poise and his experience was crucial, especially alongside the young and developing McFarland. Mackay led by example and Brian would reflect in later years that the signing of the barrel-chested Scot was one of the best of his career.

Derby clinched promotion to the First Division in 1969. Looking back, Brian would say that he'd never known a collective spirit stronger than the one created at Derby around that time. After a bit of a slow start in that promotion season, things really kicked-off when the Rams beat Stockport

County 5–1 in a League Cup tie in September 1968. Alan Hinton scored four of them and my favourite player, Kevin Hector, got the other one. Kevin was on the scoresheet twice for the next game, a 3–1 league win at home to Aston Villa. The League Cup gave Derby the opportunity to pit their wits and skills against a First Division side, Chelsea. After a goalless draw at Stamford Bridge, it was a truly memorable night when Derby won the replay 3–1. You could feel the Baseball Ground shake from the celebrations and it was clear that great things lay ahead for this Derby side.

The sense of excitement continued to grow across the city. Everyone was happy to get out of bed each Monday morning and go to work. They were already looking forward to the following Saturday. Brian used to say that Derby was a more productive city when the team was doing well. Although promotion to the First Division was secured that season, there was personal sadness for me because my Dad was not able to see them actually win it. He died in March 1969 before promotion was sealed the following month.

Dad's death from a brain haemorrhage was a tremendous shock to me. He was in his early sixties and hadn't been ill before it happened – in fact he had been counting down the days to his retirement. That's all he could talk about because he said it would give him more time to pursue his hobbies, like competing and judging at caged bird shows. I've still got a photo of him with some of the trophies he won. He also kept greyhounds, which were very well looked after. Everything was absolutely spot-on for them; they had all they could ever need. I used to think that their kennels were more comfortable than the house!

Dad was an intelligent man but he didn't get his chances in life and didn't get to Grammar School. After being a storekeeper at Rolls Royce he returned to working back down the mine. I continued to encourage him to watch football again and managed to get tickets to take him to the FA Cup Final at Wembley in 1968. As I've mentioned, it was my first FA

Cup Final and I secured some of the best seats, thanks to a friend in the Nottinghamshire FA. I took him to some Derby games and he used to enjoy coming to the players' entrance at the Baseball Ground and picking up the tickets I had arranged to collect. Not long after Brian became manager, my Dad wrote to him to say how impressed he was with the football he was now watching. Brian wrote back with a personally signed letter, dated 20 December, 1967:

"Dear Mr Shields,

Thank you for your letter, please find enclosed herewith one seat ticket for our match against Leeds United on Wednesday, 17 January.

I think that anybody who has been a supporter of Derby County for forty-five years deserves a break so we will stand the cost of the seat.

I hope you enjoy the match and thank you for your good wishes.

Yours sincerely, Brian Clough"

I can still remember the last time I saw Dad, after we'd travelled on the bus to a league match at Carlisle. My brother Trevor was with us and it was a bitterly cold night. A goal from Kevin Hector had warmed us up a bit, but we were glad to get on the coach to head back after a 1–1 draw. The bus dropped him off at Alfreton, while Trevor and I stayed on board to continue the last bit of the journey. We said goodnight to him before going our separate ways to get home. He died just a couple of days later.

Dad would have been so proud of what Derby achieved in the next few years. Having won promotion, there was great anticipation about what the new season in the First Division would bring. Although it started with a goalless draw against Burnley, the fans were not left disappointed as they went on to watch their team beat the likes of Manchester United, Liverpool and Spurs. A fourth-placed finish certainly could not be sniffed at. I felt I wanted to be a real part of this Derby success, so I joined what was known as The 100 Club. It was open to the first 100 members who joined and it gave me a few perks and privileges. For a start, it got me into the ground without queuing. I'd meet my mates first and they used to think it was funny that I was dressed in a shirt and tie for a football match. Yes, The 100 Club was that special – we even had our own ties! I'd go and have a drink in the little private bar under the stand and then sit with my mates for the match. Another drink would be waiting for me at half-time. Looking back, it seems very basic nowadays. But it was a big step forward at the time. I suppose it was the early days of match-day hospitality.

The 100 Club also involved specially arranged transport to away matches. It meant that I got the best choice of tickets and was entered into a £100 prize draw. It was a very enjoyable way to watch football. It was enjoyment that I wanted others to share. As there was a restriction on the number of people who could join The 100 Club, Ron Stevenson and I insti-gated the opening of a private bar for supporters on match-days. It was upstairs at the Baseball Hotel, where I assured the landlord there would be no trouble. It was so close to the ground that you could see the turnstiles for the Osmaston Stand from the window. As word got around, its popu-larity grew quickly and the room soon became packed. We charged five bob for membership and the money went to the Nottingham branch of the supporters club. But when the club found out about the success of this bar, they decided to stop the supporters club running it and proceeded to take it over. The same thing had happened with our supporters club trips to away matches. Ron and I organised trains for the fans so they could get to the games in style and comfort. We hired the train from British Rail and arranged to supply our own refreshments. It made a lot of money for the supporters club. We even received letters of thanks from British Rail for leaving the trains in such a clean and tidy condition. But again, when the club saw how popular these trips were, they stopped us running them and took it over themselves. We felt we had been brushed aside while they capitalised on all our good work. It left us feeling very despondent.

Thankfully, on the pitch, there was no sense of despondency. The team was going from strength to strength and went on to win the First Division title in 1972. I was working for the Co-op Bakery in Nottingham at the time and remember joining my colleagues in the yard to listen to the radio on the night that the Championship was secured. In their final game of the season, the Rams had beaten Liverpool 1–0 at the Baseball Ground thanks to a John McGovern goal. Derby were now one point clear – but both Liverpool and Leeds had a game left and could overtake them. Even though their rivals had away games (Liverpool at Arsenal and Leeds at Wolves), the odds seemed stacked against Derby.

Eventually the news came through that Liverpool had drawn and Leeds had lost, so Derby had won the title. The players learned of it during their end-of season break in Majorca and Brian found out while on holiday on the Scilly Isles. I heard it on a little transistor radio in the bakery yard.

The appeal of European football quickly captured my imagination the following season. For me, one of the highlights was in October 1973 when Benfica came to town. The atmosphere that night was incredible and the noise from the fans in a packed Baseball Ground was defeaning. I remember the groundsman had needed to put loads of sand on the pitch because Brian had watered it a little too much (the story goes that he fell asleep while the hosepipe continued to gush gallons of water onto the turf one night). I think the groundsman misheard and put seventy tonnes of sand on the pitch, instead of 17! But whatever the state of the pitch, Benfica – including the great Eusebio – could not handle what Derby threw at them that night. A 3–0 victory was fully deserved, with goals from McFarland, Hector and McGovern.

For the return leg, I travelled to Lisbon with some mates and found myself in quite an awkward situation. We were in a restaurant and I ordered lobster. It was absolutely delicious, but there was soon a bad taste in my mouth when the bill arrived. I hadn't realised that the price was per kilo, not per lobster. My mates, who had started calling me 'Cloughie' because of my admiration of Brian (and the fact I could mimic his voice quite well), thought it was hilarious. "Hey Cloughie, how are you going to pay for that, then?" they laughed, making the most of my misfortune. I refused to pay the bill and the restaurant staff called security officials over to see me. My mates wouldn't let it rest. "You're in a bit of trouble now, Cloughie, how are you going to get out of this one?" Thankfully, after a few minutes, I was able to reach an amicable agreement with the restaurant (with the timely assistance of one of my friends). But I was determined to 'get one back' on my mates who continued to give me some stick.

When we got back to the hotel, my room-mate Johnnie Birch decided to have a shower. Now was my moment. I took a pile of my clothes off the bed and hung them over the balcony, along with a towel. I then squeezed under the bed and hid. When Johnnie came into the bedroom I could hear him walk to the balcony and back again. "Cloughie, where are you?" Silence. "Hey, Cloughie, don't mess about – where are you?" More silence. "Oh my God," he said. "He's gone over the balcony." I then heard him pick up the phone to speak to our mates in the room below. "I think Cloughie's gone over the balcony – his clothes are here, but I can't see him." Johnnie quickly got dressed and joined the others. After a few minutes to let them stew, I crawled from under the bed and phoned them – using my Cloughie voice. One of them answered straight away.

"Now then, young man," I said, emphasising each word.

"Hell, it's Brian Clough on the phone," I heard one of them tell the others.

I continued my wind-up: "I hear you're Derby County fans staying in the hotel – why don't you all join me in the bar for a drink? Say, ten minutes."

I put the phone down and prepared for the final part of my joke. You can probably imagine their faces when, fully expecting to meet the great Brian Clough, they saw me walking towards them.

The match itself, in front of 75,000 people in Benfica's Stadium of Light, was a goal-less draw. Then, after victory over Spartak Trnava, came the first leg of the semi-final against Juventus in April 1973. Derby lost the first match in Turin 3–1, but it wasn't the result that angered Brian, it was the nature of it. Archie Gemmill and Roy McFarland were both booked for seemingly no good reason – and just by coincidence they were the two players who had already been cautioned in the tournament and would miss the second leg. The match at the Baseball Ground was goalless and the whole affair led to Brian famously referring to the Italians as 'cheating ba*!@*ds.' That was Brian, he always spoke as he saw things – even though it probably cost him the England job in later years. Although Derby were now out of Europe, the club was about to be at the centre of more controversy involving Brian.

*　　*　　*

I had been working on the night shift at the Co-op Bakery when I returned home and heard news which left me completely stunned. My daughter came into the bedroom and told me that Brian had resigned as Derby manager. Suddenly, it seemed that my world had collapsed. I knew that Brian and Peter's relationship with the club's board had been deteriorating, but I never thought it would lead to them both quitting. The now well-documented feud between the chairman Sam Longson and Brian had reached its peak. Longson wanted Brian to cut down on his media work, yet the chairman had been lapping up all the publicity and success that Brian had brought to the club. He couldn't get enough of it. No longer was Longson going to Barnsley and Bradford, he was enjoying the hospitality of the Manchester United boardroom. Yet the very thing that was putting Derby on the map was the same thing he was trying to throttle.

I felt incensed by it all. Derby had been doing so well and now it was all falling apart. I wanted to do something about it. I joined the Protest Movement, which aimed to get Brian and Peter re-instated and I used my links with the supporters club to get more fans involved and informed. Through the Movement, I met Michael Keeling again – he had come to our branch meeting with Brian and Peter in Nottingham. Michael resigned as a Derby County director in protest at the way Brian was being treated, but with hindsight he should have stayed to fight from within. Michael knew Brian well and over the years we became the very best of friends. To help the campaign, Michael sold some of his shares to supporters he knew. I was encouraged to buy one and, as a result, a group of us owned one share each in the club. It meant that we were officially registered as shareholders and it felt like a big step forward. We had a foot in the door. At meetings, the directors' 'inner sanctum' would suddenly be invaded by this group of fans. We sat there, listening to the meeting and voting. We had a spokesman, Michael Dickinson, who was very eloquent and could challenge some of the things the members of the board were saying about Brian. The Movement gave us some hope, but the directors had lawyers speaking for them and it was always going to be a huge challenge for us to succeed.

In an effort to show the support Brian had from fans, I was interviewed on television as part of the campaign. Other members of the Movement knew I had good contacts among the supporters and asked if I could rally more people to back the cause. At times, that seemed easier said than done. Some supporters I spoke to, including my friends, said we were simply fans and there was nothing we could do about it. But I felt it was all an injustice – not just for Brian but for the fans as well. The more I heard about what the board was saying about Brian, the more I felt supporters would agree that something should be done. I helped to raise funds for the legal side of the campaign by helping to organise various events such as dances and it was through that work I met Brian again, along with his wife Barbara and the players.

I went to several meetings of the Protest Movement, including one at the Kings Hall when there was a lot of gossip about a man sitting at the back, in the shadows. There were whispers that it was a spy from the club. But it later emerged that it was actually Brian – and he made a quick exit when he suspected he had been spotted. In my desperation to find any way I could to campaign for Brian's re-instatement, I joined what was known as the Executive Club. I hoped I could pull a few strings behind the scenes. For just a few pounds extra, the Executive Club ran special trips to away matches – I would travel first class on the train alongside directors and other executives. I thought that if I could get amongst that group of people, I might be able to use some influence to secure Brian's return. But it was like trying to fight your way through a brick wall.

A protest march was held through the streets of Derby and I made sure that I was part of it. It was held before a home match against Leicester. There was a fantastic atmosphere during the march, with people carrying placards and banners, but I think there should have been a bigger turnout. If eighty per cent of the fans who turned out for the game that afternoon had taken part in the march beforehand it would have had such a big impact. While we were walking through the streets behind the band, on-lookers were shouting at us 'Why don't you grow up?' and 'You're being stupid –it's nothing to do with you!' They seemed steeped in the old attitude that you can't do anything – that you couldn't try to change things.

There was talk of the players possibly going on strike. They wanted to get involved in the campaign, but they remained very professional and their role as players came first. The minute that Dave MacKay returned to become manager, we knew we were finished. I think Brian was devastated when Dave took the job. My life had been built around Derby County and I continued to watch them, even without Brian as manager. There was still some wonderful football to enjoy and they went on to win the title in 1974. I watched them play again in the European Cup and cheered them to a fantastic 4–1 first leg victory at home to Real Madrid in October 1975. For the return leg in the Bernebau Stadium the following month, I was part of the club's VIP guests and still have a copy of the official itinerary we received. The England manager Don Revie was also on the list of VIP's. I stayed at the Hotel Luz Palacio and before the game, there was a sight-seeing tour of Madrid and a pre-match dinner at 7pm before transport was provided to the game, which kicked-off at 9pm. Back home it was Bonfire Night – but unfortunately in Madrid Derby got their fingers burned that night, losing 5–1 in front of a tremendous crowd of around 120,000.

Even then, it seemed to me that nothing could compare with the time when Brian walked into the Baseball Ground. No team in the country had experienced anything like the kind of transformation and sudden success Derby had enjoyed. So it's no wonder there was such a feeling of desolation when Brian and Peter resigned. Brian always regretted resigning from Derby – he said it was the daftest thing he ever did. He said he should have remained at the club and beaten them. It could all have been so different.

*   *   *

Although Brian had left, I stayed in contact with Michael Keeling, who had remained a good friend of Brian's. Michael invited me to watch Nottingham Forest at the City Ground, where Brian had become manager. I liked what I saw at Forest and continued to watch them when Derby were playing away. Before the games, I would have a meal with Michael and his friends at the Italian restaurant on Trent Bridge. It became a regular fixture for me.

Michael would phone me to say, "I've got you a ticket for the guest room at Forest, see you there." I loved the hospitality at the ground. I would pay for the match ticket and then go along to the guest room afterwards and saw some of the VIP's. I was so impressed with the football I was seeing that I decided to buy a season ticket at the City Ground. You may think that's strange for a Derby supporter, but I'd remained a huge admirer of Brian and I wanted to be part of what he was building at Forest.

For a couple of years I had a season ticket at both Forest and Derby. My heart was at Derby but it was being torn apart by what I was seeing at Forest. It was hurting me inside because I still regarded them as the old enemy. Brian was well aware that I had a season ticket at both clubs, but eventually I gave up my ticket at Derby with a broken heart and became a fully-fledged Forest supporter. I was called a traitor by my Derby friends because I was transferring to the 'enemy'. I got some serious stick from them. I was treated like a blackleg, like someone who had broken a strike. I stood down from my role with the supporters club. That came as a blow to my colleagues in the branch, especially the secretary who still wanted me to go and see Derby matches when I could. I had to explain to him that I loved what I was seeing at Forest. After the matches, I would go into the guest room at the City Ground and enjoy the company of managers and former players. The whole experience was first class. It seemed a bit like The 100 Club I had joined at Derby – but the additional hospitality I received at Forest made it much better. I felt that I was being sucked into a wonderful whirlwind of success and excitement, all orchestrated by Brian Clough. I gave up a fantastic relationship with all the people at Derby – but this was the influence that Brian was starting to have on me.

3.

At The Team Hotel

The phone rang and it was Michael Keeling. "Would you like to come with us to Leicester on Saturday? Forest are playing there."

It was September 1977 and an invitation too good to turn down. I agreed and met Michael at a hotel, near junction 25 of the M1 at Sandiacre, to make our way to the game. It was then I realised that we weren't simply going to the match; we were heading for the Forest team hotel, the Holiday Inn at Leicester. We walked in and I was soon among the Forest team and backroom staff. It was a fantastic opportunity for an ordinary supporter like me. I felt as if I was floating on a cloud.

A few minutes went by and then Michael told me that Brian wanted some Mannequins – the small cigars – and that I should take them up to his room. So I went up there, feeling very apprehensive, and knocked on the door. It wasn't long before the door opened and I was face-to-face with my football hero.

"I've brought these for you, Mr Clough," were the few words I could manage, as I passed him the cigars.

"My name's Brian," he replied. "And I'll sort the money out with you when I come back down."

Now feeling on top of the world, I went back downstairs and we all had lunch together before the match and then prepared to leave. As the team was getting on the coach, Brian was at the hotel reception and a Leicester fan came up to him, pestering him. I said to the man, "Would you mind not bothering Mr Clough, he's got a big job to do today. You'll have another opportunity some other time."

So he agreed and left him alone. Brian then turned round towards his support staff and said: "'Ere you lot, this man looks after me – he's my new minder."

And that reputation stuck with me for quite a while. After the game, which Forest won 3–0, Brian got off the team coach at Sandiacre, where he met Michael and I before Michael took him back to his house in Derbyshire.

As if things couldn't get any better, I was soon invited to Brian's home on Ferrers Way in Derby. His three children were there and I remember talking to his daughter, Elizabeth. She was a little girl then and was sitting on the carpet reading one of her Dad's scripts for a television commercial. The script was written for Brian and Peter, so Elizabeth and I proceeded to each take a role and read the lines. I read Peter's part and Elizabeth was Brian. I'm not sure if the script was ever developed into a proper advert, but I was thrilled about the whole visit. Simply meeting his family in those circumstances was a great privilege.

As my friendship with Brian developed, I was allowed to travel on the team coach. That, too, was a huge privilege because Brian wouldn't even allow the directors to travel with him. He didn't like them interfering with his work. In fact, there was an occasion when I was chatting to him in his office and the chairman walked in. Brian let rip at him. "I knock before I go into your office, so you can do the same for me," he said. So the chairman walked out and after a few moments of silence there was a knock at the door. Brian snapped: "Who is it?" "It's the chairman," came the reply. "Well you better come in then." I didn't know where to look, I felt so embarrassed for the chairman. But it was Brian's way of showing that he was the boss. Within a few minutes they were laughing and the incident had been forgotten.

On the days I travelled on the coach, it was my job to pick-up the news-papers and chocolates for the team, for when we were coming back from a game. Sometimes I'd meet the coach at the Swallow Hotel near junction 28 of the M1 and my arms would be full of all the papers and sweets. I would always bring a few boxes of pork pies as well, because I worked for Pork Farms. It was in the days before meals were provided on the bus and the players would tuck into the pork pies during the journey back. Brian would usually have one too. Peter Taylor used to tell me, "While they keep winning, you must keep bringing those pies!" I continued to do that until Albert the driver told me not to bring any more. He said the players were just eating the meat and then chucking the pastry down the toilet onboard the coach. Admittedly, it was very rich pastry! When Brian heard that the toilet was being blocked with all the pastry, he decided to have the loo taken out. After that, I think the players had to cross their legs for the journeys to and from games! But later, after Forest won the First Division title, the club invested in a new £50,000 luxury team coach, which was a 'state of the art' vehicle at that time. There were twenty-two reclining seats for the players, a couple of tables for playing cards, plus a hospitality area, a heating system and sun-tinted windows.

There was a strict protocol on the coach. Brian would sit behind the driver and Michael and I would sit on the other side of the aisle, also at the front. I'd often perch on the little seat near the steps, so I could chat to Albert the driver, whom Brian affectionately called 'Old Man'. On good days, when Forest had won, Brian would have a laugh with us and he'd be singing some Frank Sinatra songs. Something like 'Nice and Easy' or 'Fly Me To The Moon' and we'd have a little sing-song with him. When meals were provided on the bus, the players would be served first. There was a curtain down the middle of the coach and the players would sit behind that. If it had been a bad day, Brian would sometimes walk down the bus, give the players a rollocking and then whip the curtain back into place. During one journey, the Forest captain and England player Stuart Pearce walked down to the front of the bus and asked if the players could have some music on. Pearcey, who loved punk rock, had a cassette or CD ready to play. "It's not your loud, heavy-metal stuff, is it?" Brian asked. "No, it's something one of the lads has brought along," replied the skipper. Albert put the music on, but it was Brian who had the final say – it was his coach.

A fine example of that concerned the defender Des Walker. We were travelling back from a game and Brian had overheard that Des wanted to get back to Nottingham in a hurry because he was going somewhere.

"Oh, does he?" said Brian. "Old Man, are we anywhere near East Midlands Airport?"

"Yes, boss," replied Albert.

"How far away are we?"

"Oh, I'd say about half an hour."

"Well, I want to go there – take us to the airport."

So Albert followed Brian's instructions and took us off the motorway and up the slip-road towards the airport.

"Just drive round here and stop," said Brian. Then he raised his voice so the players could hear.

"Hey, you lot. Get your passports ready. In a couple of weeks we'll be coming here for a lovely holiday in the sunshine."

Then he turned round and added: "Right, Albert, take us back home and drive steady."

As you can imagine, Des was now wound-up like a coiled spring. We had been making good time on our way home, but Brian's airport detour had added three-quarters of an hour on to the journey. Brian was in a good mood – he'd simply done it to wind-up Des.

There were also times when Brian knew how to build-up a player's confidence, when it was least expected. Back in March 1992, Forest endured a disaster at Portsmouth, where they lost 1–0 and were knocked out of the FA Cup. The goalkeeper, Mark Crossley, had been in a bit of trouble the night before and, as he got on the coach, he was clearly feeling down about what had happened that afternoon. I heard Brian tell him: "Hey you, get your head off the floor. It happens to all of us – get your feet up and relax."

But there was another occasion when Brian's mood was quite the opposite and I was on the wrong end of it. I'd got on the team coach at the City Ground and sat in my usual seat next to Michael Keeling. Brian saw me and – in earshot of everyone else – said to me, "I didn't know you were coming today." A few moments later, he had a right go at me.

"Shields, if you ever get on my coach again without my knowledge and without my permission, I'll kick your backside across Nottingham and you'll never travel on this coach again!"

Initially, I felt so embarrassed that he had said this in front of everyone, that my face must have gone bright red and I sank into my seat, hoping it would just swallow me up and I'd disappear.

I turned to Michael. "Didn't you tell him I was coming?" I asked him quietly.

"Of course I did," said Michael. "He's just got a lot on his mind at the moment."

The coach set-off and after about twenty minutes I had a word with Albert. I now felt so incensed by the way Brian had spoken to me in front of everyone else.

"Where did you put my bag, Albert?"

"Why Colin, what's the matter?" Albert replied.

"Because I want to get off."

"Oh no you're not," said Albert. "You just stay put."

Albert was brilliant. He calmed me down and told me not to be silly. He said it was just Brian's way. When the coach reached the team hotel, Brian changed his tune. Pointing to me, he spoke to the coach Liam O'Kane: "See my mate there, he must have the biggest headache of all time. Look after him, make sure he gets anything he wants – the best room, the lot."

It was Brian's way of apologising without saying anything to me. I didn't need the best room, and didn't get it, but the sentiment was there. At first, I didn't understand why he had spoken to me so angrily in the first place. Why had he torn a strip off me? But looking back, I don't think he wanted it to appear to everyone else that he didn't know who was on his bus. After all, he wouldn't even let the chairman on board!

Albert became a good friend over the years. We would spend many hours talking during the long journeys. He got on really well with Brian too. Brian wasn't a good passenger – in a car, on a coach or on a plane. So driving the coach could be a stressful job. During a trip to a game in Norfolk, Albert got a little lost and I thought to myself, "Albert, this doesn't look good." There was a diversion at Sutton Bridge and Albert had driven down a road which seemed to go on forever. It eventually became a cart track. I could see him fidgeting in his seat, as if things were not quite right.

All of a sudden, Brian's voice rose behind us: "Hey, Old Man, are you bloody lost?"

"I'm alright boss – I've just got to turn round," said Albert. I really felt some sympathy for him in that situation. He was well and truly lost, but he got us to the right place eventually.

I could see at first-hand that being the driver of the team coach was a big responsibility and could be very difficult at times. Some grounds could be tricky to drive into, especially West Ham's Upton Park. That visit always involved one hell of a tight manoeuvre. I could see Albert getting stressed, concentrating, as he guided the bus into the narrowest of spaces. Brian said: "Old Man, get a fag on."

Albert loved a smoke. "Thanks boss," he said and quickly lit a cigarette to calm himself down.

One of the players shouted, jokingly: "You snivvelling bxxxxxx, Albert" because he'd said 'Thanks boss,' to Brian. Everyone was laughing, including Albert. But he was always the professional and got the coach through the tightest of spots and parked up. During one of the pre-season breaks in Cala Millor in Majorca, we took Albert along, with some of the team. Everyone liked him and the players loved him. That's why I was determined to make sure he was alright when his health took a turn for the worst.

I was with the team in a hotel in Croydon and we were stopping there for one night before a match. On the morning of the game, I heard a knock on my door. It was one of Brian's backroom staff, Alan Hill, and he told me that Albert had been taken ill. We went into his bedroom and he didn't look at all well. When an ambulance arrived, I went with him to the hospital. When we got there, I told the hospital staff that I would let his family know and asked the medics not to make any details public knowledge. I made sure Albert was comfortable in the hospital, got hold of his home phone number and told him that I would contact his wife.

I got back to the hotel by taxi and arrangements were made for a replacement coach driver – it would be Tony, who had driven the directors bus down to a neighbouring hotel. He was brought over to where the team was staying and Brian said to me: "Now then, Col. You sit with Tony and look after him." I knew all the directions, so I had the special responsibility of ensuring the team bus got to the ground and back home safely. Remember, there were no sat-navs in those days. In fact, I was known as 'The Navigator' because I knew the way to all the football grounds. From that point onwards, I used all the knowledge I had picked-up from Albert over the years. I told Tony which grounds were difficult to get into, at what point the Police outriders would be joining us as we got closer to a stadium, and which stewards were always awkward. Understandably, on that first morning of driving the team coach, Tony was very nervous. Anyone would be in that position. When he'd driven the directors down a few hours earlier, the last thing he expected was to be taking a coach full of football stars to the ground and back home.

A few days after that match in London, the Forest chairman Maurice Roworth saw me and made a point of expressing his gratitude for how I'd handled things, especially for looking after Albert. Maurice called me into his office and I'll never forget what he told me. "I want to thank you on behalf of Nottingham Forest for what you did last Saturday," he said. "And to tell you that you'll always be welcome at this club as an honoured guest. You are a friend of the club for life." I thanked him for the kind gesture and told him I'd been proud and pleased to help.

Tony was a very capable driver and an extremely nice man. He became the regular driver of the team coach and I would navigate, with Brian sitting just behind us. Soon after Tony had got the job on the team bus, I remember we were on the A5 when a car suddenly pulled out towards us. For a split second, it startled Tony and the bus jolted slightly. As I've mentioned, Brian was a terrible passenger – and he let rip.

"Don't you realise you've got a coach full of millions of pounds worth of players here?" he shouted.

I tried to reassure Tony and told him that he would get used to Brian as a passenger. I think Tony was quite upset about what had happened so, referring to Brian, I tried to make him feel better – just like Albert had done with me. "He's quite strung-up," I told Tony. "He's got a big game on this afternoon. Just try to tolerate him for the time being. He'll be right as rain soon." And, sure enough, he was. Over time, Brian and Tony got on really well. Brian made sure he looked after him. Tony admired Brian and he loved his job. In fact he continued driving the coach after Brian retired and I'm pleased to say Tony and I remain good friends.

Brian always recognised the important job the Police were doing when they escorted us in and out of football grounds. If we were leaving a ground on the coach, Brian would tell the club secretary, Paul White, to give the Police outriders a tip, something like £50. At a suitable stopping point, the boss of the out-riders would climb on to the coach and say: "Thank you very much, Mr Clough." And he would always reply: "Hey, thanks a lot for what you're doing too."

If we were staying in a hotel, sometimes Brian would be mischievous and take me to where the players were eating. He would turn to me and say:

"Now then, which one was it, Col?"

"What do you mean, Brian?" I'd reply, wary of what he was about to say.

"Who was it that was calling me a big head last night?"

The players would all look at each other, wondering what was coming next. It would really put me on the spot and I would have to think fast in order to diffuse the situation.

"He's not here, Brian," I'd reply.

I used to stand my corner with him and he'd say: "Ah, alright then, Col. If you say so."

Brian was just keeping everyone on their toes, but it was also his way of showing the players that I could be trusted. I can imagine they might have been thinking, "Who's that little bugger with Brian? What's he up to?" But the players knew I wasn't going to snitch on them about anything. I never would. We would be staying at hotels and playing pool and Brian would say: "My mate here can beat the lot of you." I was quite handy at pool and the lads liked it if I beat Archie Gemmill, who was very competitive at everything. It was all good fun. I got on well with the players and many of them would say good morning to me when they got on the coach.

"The players like you," Brian told me. "Everybody likes you. You never stick your nose in and you don't give it all that ..." (he would raise his right hand as if he was making a puppet speak). And he added: "I can depend on you." It was a great complement.

I even joined the players for a bit of a kick-about when we were staying in East Anglia before a game. I wasn't wearing football boots, in fact I'd got my proper black formal shoes on. The lads were passing the ball to me and I was having a few shots on goal. The next minute, I heard some activity behind me and suddenly looked down. The defender, Brian Laws, was wrapping some string round the bottom of my legs.

"What are you doing?" asked one of the other players.

"I'm tying his legs together because we can't stop him," replied Lawsy. It was the type of fun that Brian encouraged occasionally to ensure the players were relaxed.

When Brian was on form, the atmosphere was completely electric. Wherever we were, the place would be buzzing. Sometimes you had to eat a bit of humble pie – like the chairman did when he failed to knock on Brian's door before entering his office. He kept everyone on their toes, including me. Sometimes it was like walking on broken glass because you never knew what he was going to do or say next. But there were many other times when you felt completely relaxed and comfortable in his company. That's how he achieved all the success he enjoyed over the years. Brian was a master of psychology. He may not have achieved academic qualifications, but that didn't matter. He used to say that if his children asked him how many O-Levels and A-Levels he had, he would get the box containing all his football medals and put it on the table. "These are my O-Levels and A-Levels," he'd say. Brian was also the most generous and thoughtful man that I've ever met. Yes, I might get an occasional telling-off but it didn't mean I respected him any less, because 99% of the time he was right (he would say he was right 100% of the time, of course). Neither did it mean that I was afraid of him. Contrary to what some people might think, he didn't rule by fear – because fear brings out the worst in people and Brian's record shows he brought out the best – the very best.

* * *

I loved it whenever Brian phoned me. But he didn't like it when he phoned my house and I was out, because he would have to leave a message on the answerphone.

"You've got that bloody answerphone on again," he would say.

"I don't like talking to those bloody machines – give me a call when you get in."

Brian and Michael would often call me to make arrangements for a match or a trip away. "What are you doing on Saturday?" was a common question. As each match-day approached, I'd be forever waiting for my phone to ring, anticipating the invitation to join them. I had a full-time job and I think Michael was careful not to pressurise me over the arrangements, in case it impinged too much on my work time. But my boss seemed to be happy with the situation and I used to look after him and my staff by arranging match tickets for them – they would get all the best seats. Brian shared things with me and I felt it was important to do the same and share things too. I also paid for four season tickets near the Directors' Box at the City Ground, to be used for myself, family and friends.

In the early days of meeting-up with Brian and Michael, my experience of technology took a giant leap forward – they suggested I should get a mobile phone in the car. I must have been among the first people in the country to have one. Both Brian and Michael had mobile phones, so they urged me to have one too, so that the three of us could keep in touch when arrangements needed to be made. I was absolutely delighted about it, because phones like that were an exciting innovation. To save me the cost of buying a new phone, Michael said I could have his and he would get another one. It was a huge thing – it sat on a box about six inches by four inches and six inches deep, with a handset and cord. You could pick it up and take it with you, but it was so big and heavy it was like carrying a suitcase around. I found a little garage near Bulwell Forest in Nottingham which specialised in fitting them into cars. The phones cost an absolute fortune to buy, so I was lucky that I got mine for nothing. The call charges were around one-pound per minute, so I didn't use it to make calls very often, even though I'd got Brian and Michael's phone numbers. They insisted on calling me.

There were many times when Michael and I would drive to an away match and then – on the way back – we would meet the coach at a designated point. Brian would get into the car and we would take him back to his home in Derbyshire. It was a fantastic feeling as Michael and I drove away from various football grounds as part of the Police escort for Forest. We would follow the team bus out of the stadium and the Police would be told that we were 'the boss' car.' We'd have to drive at top speed as the Police outriders guided us through all the traffic which had been brought to a standstill. It made your adrenalin pump as much as the ninety minutes of football!

There were also occasions when we would take Brian in the car rather than go on the team bus. I once drove Brian's big Mercedes back from Villa Park – that was a big responsibility and I'm glad to say it was an uneventful journey. It was rare that Brian would drive us – but when we were travelling in his car we weren't allowed to touch any of the controls on the dashboard, including the radio. "Our Simon's set it for the football results," he'd say. Neither were we allowed to alter the heating controls. He loved to have the air conditioning blasting away. We would be sitting there in overcoats, while Brian would be in his T-shirt and shorts.

One afternoon we were travelling in the car into the Knightsbridge area of London, heading for a hotel near the Royal Albert Hall. Michael was driving and went the wrong way and I told him he had taken a wrong turning. Brian didn't hear me – but then suddenly there was the familiar voice from the back seat.

"Hey Keeling, you're on the wrong road!"

Michael didn't drop me in it and I said: "We're alright, Brian, we'll be OK."

But that wasn't the end of it – Brian was obviously getting fed-up and he told me to keep quiet. "You're supposed to be the navigator – that's all you're here for. And we're lost!"

So I turned to Michael and said quietly: "Just turn round here and we'll get back on track. It won't be a problem."

When we arrived at the hotel where the team was staying, Brian asked the coach, Liam O'Kane, whether he had got any aspirins.

"What's the matter, boss, have you got a headache?" asked Liam. "No," replied Brian, but pointing to me, he added: "He has – I've just given him a right ear-full."

On the day Forest won the 1977–78 league title with a goalless draw at Coventry, Michael and I had travelled to Highfield Road in the car, picking-up Brian's journalist friend Vince Wilson on the way. They always looked after us well at Coventry and after the match we enjoyed a glass of champagne. Everyone was absolutely elated. We took Vince back to the railway station and then had to double-back in the car to meet Brian at the Posthouse Hotel at Sandiacre, which was a regular meeting place. The team coach had reached the hotel before us and Brian had found some-where quiet to sit and wait for us, away from public attention. When we arrived, the receptionist told us where he was. Michael took Brian home and I waved them off before driving home too, still pinching myself that I'd just witnessed such a significant day in Forest's history.

I'm fortunate to say there were many more memorable days. It was a very special feeling to walk into football grounds alongside Brian. It made me feel ten feet tall, even though (as I've said before) I'm quite a short chap. I felt particularly honoured when Brian asked me to look after the former Liverpool manager Bill Shankly before an away match against Liverpool.

We were about to have lunch in the hotel before the game and Brian said: "Col, I'd like you to look after Mr Shankly for me, make sure he's OK." I couldn't believe I was sitting next to another managerial legend. Mr Shankly dined with us at the hotel and I got on very well with him. He was easy to chat to. We'd both been miners so I guess we had something in common. We talked about football and after the game Brian made a point of saying how much he appreciated what I had done. As we drove home he said: "Col, I've got to thank you for looking after my mate today. They're not treating him right at Liverpool after all he's done for them. But he's had a good day with us. Well done."

Bill Shankly came to see other Forest matches after that. I was standing near the door in the guest room at the City Ground when he came in. I was delighted to see him walk over to me. In his gruff Scottish voice he said: "Hello son, how is he? Are you looking after him?" He was referring to Brian of course. I told Mr Shankly that it was lovely to see him again and that everything was fine. He responded with a smile: "Well done, keep looking after him, he's a good man."

I also looked after another of Brian's VIP's – the widow of Harry Storer, the man who was essentially Brian and Peter Taylor's mentor. Brian had huge admiration for Harry, who had been manager at Coventry City, Birmingham City and Derby County. Although Brian's manager at Sunderland, Alan Brown, was also a massive influence on his career, there is no doubt he had a great deal of respect for Harry and the way he went about things. A lot of Brian's attitude to the game came from Harry: that sense of 'my word is the last one – and no-one questions it.' Whenever Mrs Storer wanted to come to a Forest match, my friends Harry Close and Eric Edwards would pick her up from Coventry and bring her to the game, and then take her back home again. I would often travel with them, but before we arrived at the City Ground we would call in to a nearby hotel so she could enjoy a quick sherry. Then we'd go into Brian's office and she would say to him: "These young men are wonderful, they look after me so well." Brian would respond: "Well, why do you think I chose them?" Mrs Storer would get the VIP treatment for the day and I have no doubt she thoroughly enjoyed it.

Another little job of mine involved looking after the families of referees and match officials. They would have their own corner in the guest room, with drinks and sandwiches provided for them. Brian would say: "Keep an eye on them for me and make sure they're looked after." It wasn't an official role for me, but Brian wanted me to check that the referee and linesmen were happy. "If they ask to see me, make sure I get the message," he would tell me. After the game, the referee would approach me, shake hands and say 'thank you' for how well they had been treated. But it was Brian who was responsible for creating such a welcoming environment for them.

Throughout his career, Brian never criticised referees. He stuck by them all the time and I think there was mutual respect. He would even fine players if they gave the officials any backchat. In an interview with the BBC's John Motson, he came to their defence and criticised those who acted as 'judge and jury' on television.

"I think what you do to referees is nothing short of criminal," he told Motson. "And I think the standard you feel should be coming from referees at the moment is absolutely incredible. I've worked in your industry as a layman and I've looked at one of your machines twenty-four times and still couldn't get it right. He (a referee) makes a decision in a few seconds, or a second, in the heat of the moment, with twenty-two players and thirty thousand people shouting and bellowing."

One of my proudest moments was meeting Jack Taylor, who became 'the referees' ref' and was in charge of the 1974 World Cup Final. He was an absolute gentleman. I'm not sure if it's true, but one of his favourite anecdotes involved a match at Luton Town when he suffered a cut to his face after being hit by a penny thrown from the crowd. The comedian Eric

Morecambe, who was a Luton director, went to see him and asked if he was alright and whether he was going to report the club for what had happened. When Taylor confirmed he wasn't going to report them, Morecambe replied: "Good, now can I have my penny back?"

It was also a pleasure to meet other referees like Leslie Shapter and Clive Thomas. The latter was a good friend of Brian's and paid a personal tribute at his memorial service. I'm glad to say that there are still some referees these days who you don't realise are there on the pitch and they don't make the headlines – that's the sign of a good ref. But unfortunately there are still some who think they are more important than what is going on around them. They try to create a name for themselves. Others make some brave decisions, when the cameras can see much more than *they* can. Brian's interview with John Motson all those years ago is still relevant today. It's unfair to judge a man on an instant decision made in the heat of the moment, when you can replay it time and time again on television. I think the officials will certainly benefit from the introduction of some limited technology. But I wouldn't want to see a situation where every decision is questioned and the match is stopping every few minutes. Yes, the referees make mistakes and sometimes there should be more consistency in their decisions from one match to another. But they're only human, they're not robots.

*　　*　　*

Over the years, I have found myself in some incredible situations, experiencing the sights and sounds of top football. I got much closer to professional football than I could ever have dreamed of. At some away matches, I would assist the backroom staff with the big skips containing the players' kit and help lay out the shirts, shorts and socks in the dressing room. We would then go out and have a look at the pitch and walk along the touchline. The pitch itself was out of bounds. We would usually see someone from the host club and the Forest staff would have a quick chat with them before we drove back to the hotel for lunch. Michael and I would sit at the same table as Brian and his staff to have something to eat. When it was time to leave to make our way to the ground, the players would gather together and the hotel staff would often line-up to wish them well as they left. It was all very civilised and friendly, with the team, in return, thanking the hotel staff and management.

The only time I was in the dressing room when the players were getting changed was for a match at Old Trafford. I looked around, absolutely fascinated to be there, at the heart of it all, as the players were preparing for the game. I'd been told that Peter Taylor had asked to see me there.

"Colin, I want you to do a job for me," said Peter. "I've got all these tickets and I want to make sure they get to the right people."

He then handed me various envelopes and explained which tickets should go to which people. But it was very difficult for me to concentrate on what he was saying because I couldn't believe I was standing in the same dressing room as the Forest players preparing for a vital match.

"Are you listening to me?" asked Peter, noticing that I wasn't giving him my full attention. "Are you sure you know what I've been talking about? I hope you've got it right!" Although he could tell I was distracted, I made sure that all the tickets got to the right people.

Another afternoon I will never forget, involved a match at Anfield, which I thought I was going to miss altogether. I had travelled there in the car with Michael, who had our tickets as well as a number of envelopes containing tickets for other people, which Brian had arranged. Eventually, Michael handed-out all the envelopes to the right people and only ours were left. But then another friend of Brian's approached us and asked for their tickets, which they said they had been promised.

"You better have these then," said Michael, realising he was going to have to hand-over the last envelope – with our tickets inside. He turned to me, looking dejected, and suggested that we should go and find somewhere to have a drink, because we weren't going to see the match. We had started to walk away from the ground when the Liverpool secretary saw us and shouted: "Michael, where are you going?" Michael explained that he had given our tickets away and we wouldn't be able to watch the game. "Come with me," was the response. "I'll sort out a seat in the Directors' Box for you." We were taken into the stand and Michael was given the last available seat in the Directors' Box. For a moment I thought my luck had run out again. But the next thing I knew, the secretary was carrying a big wicker chair for me. He took it to the front of the box and placed it between the Liverpool chairman and the Forest chairman. And that's where I sat for the entire match, right on the front row. It was incredible - a fantastic experience. The same can be said for the match I spent sitting on the Forest bench.

Brian's secretary, Carole, walked over to me before a sell-out game at the City Ground against his former club, Leeds United. "The boss wants a word with you," said Carole, so I followed her to his office.

"Col, I've got a problem – perhaps you can help me out?" asked Brian.

"Well, I'll do my best," I replied, not knowing what I might be committing myself to.

"Can I use your season tickets? There isn't a spare seat anywhere in the ground and I've got some people in mind who need tickets for the game."

"Of course you can, Brian," I said, wondering if this meant I was going to miss the game altogether.

"Col, thank you. I suppose the only problem now is where you're going to sit."

There was silence for a moment before Brian added:

"Will you sit on the bench with our Des?"

I almost fell through the floor. I couldn't believe what Brian had just suggested. The idea of sitting on the Forest bench for an entire match was too good an opportunity to turn down. Brian could see from my reaction of pure astonishment that I was more than happy to oblige.

"You'll be OK, Jimmy will look after you," he added, referring to the Forest trainer, Jimmy Gordon.

As the Forest players ran out of the tunnel, Brian's brother Des and I waited just behind them. Then we took our places on the bench, next to the dugout. I didn't dare look round into the crowd in case any of my mates could see me. I wasn't the type of person to make a song and dance about having such a fantastic opportunity at the time – Brian wouldn't have liked me to do that and neither was it in my nature to behave like that anyway.

As the match was about to get underway, Des lit a cigarette. "Mr Clough, you canna smoke here." It was the gruff Scottish accent of Jimmy Gordon. "I'm afraid it's not allowed here – this is where we work."

I will never forget sitting there, so close to the action that I could hear every crunching tackle and every thud of boot against bone. Although I have played football and I have watched it from the stands, I had never appreciated the sheer physicality of the professional game, until then. How some of those players left the field with all four limbs intact I will never know. Some of the challenges were incredibly tough and it made me real-ise how unjust it can be when fans shout abuse at some players for lying injured on the ground. After the game, I thanked Brian for giving me such a once-in-a-lifetime experience. I had thoroughly enjoyed it – although I still prefer to watch from the stands, looking down on the players, as if looking at the pieces of a chessboard. Most of the time, while sitting on the bench, it was like looking through a sea of legs. It was hard to work out the positions of the players. But it made me admire Brian even more for what he did during games, assessing positional play even though he sat at the same level as the pitch.

On another occasion, Brian invited me to share my opinions with some of the top names in the world of football management at the time.

I had dropped him off in the car for a meeting of the League Managers Association at Coventry City's Highfield Road stadium. I was going to a nearby trade exhibition for my work. Afterwards, I returned to Highfield Road to pick Brian up and waited in reception for him. The next thing I knew, Coventry's Jimmy Hill came into the reception area and turned towards me.

"Have you come to collect Mr Clough?" he asked. When I confirmed that was why I was waiting, Jimmy added: "Well, he wants you to join us."

I accompanied Jimmy along the corridors and was invited to join all the managers for lunch. Within a few minutes I was sitting alongside Brian, Graham Kelly of the Football Association, the West Ham manager John Lyall and Ron Saunders, who managed Aston Villa before joining Birmingham City and then West Brom. They were discussing the relation-ship between players and fans. Signalling to me, Brian told them: "Why don't you listen to my mate here, about what he thinks. He's a fan on the terraces. He'll tell you." So they involved me in this conversation and it went really well. I felt on top of the world – to think these influential people were listening to what I thought. Among the other big names at the event was Sir Matt Busby. We all had a photograph together and I was standing in the middle of them – but it's one of my big regrets that I can't get hold of a copy. I think it is in the archives somewhere. Maybe one day it will re-surface as a reminder of a truly remarkable day.

That afternoon in Coventry was not the only time when Brian asked for my opinion. Sometimes I would go down to the City Ground on a Sunday morning when Brian would be talking things over with his backroom staff. The chairman would be there as well. He would ask what I thought about the previous day's game and I would sink into my seat. I really didn't like being asked for my opinion in those situations. I told Brian I didn't have the technical knowledge to comment on things like that. But I took it as a great complement that he would ask me. The same thing often happened in the most unlikely of circumstances. We would be travelling in the car and he would say:

"Col, who was our best player?" If there were other people with us I would think to myself, "Oh, don't do this to me Brian." I felt it was a bit embarrassing because I wasn't professionally involved in football. "I didn't see a bad one today," I'd reply, trying to be diplomatic. But when we were on our own in the car, I'd tell him – and it was usually a certain Number Nine.

4.

The Number Nine

Many years before Brian's son Nigel became a household name in his own right, as one of England's leading strikers, he and my youngest son David would have a kickabout at the City Ground. They were young boys in those days and their mini-matches weren't played-out on the pitch, they would be emulating their heroes in a concrete space under the Main Stand. After each home game, when the fans had left the stadium, you could hear the echo of their football bouncing from one direction to the other. Then, once their game was over, Brian would arrange for them to share fish and chips together in a private room near his office.

But after one game, against Liverpool, the after-match routine did not go to plan and Brian asked to see me urgently. I was in the guest room at the City Ground and Brian's secretary, Carole, said to me: "The boss wants you." So I went to his office.

"Where's your lad," asked Brian, getting straight to the point.

"He's with your lad," I replied, wondering what was coming next.

"Well, where's that then – where are our lads?" Brian was becoming more agitated.

"I don't know, Brian." I didn't know what else to say, but I could see he was not happy about it.

"Well, it's his fault," he said, referring to David.

Trying to smooth things over, and hoping the pair would not be too far away, I told Brian:

"I'll try and find them," and quickly left his office.

I went to look under the Main Stand, where they would usually be playing football. There was no sign of them. After a little while, they both turned up, with David looking at me very sheepishly.

Brian wanted to know where they had been and I think there was a vow of silence between the two boys. Neither lad wanted to get the other one into trouble. It transpired that, purely out of curiosity, they had followed the Liverpool fans out of the stadium, as the Police were escorting them. I think the boys had walked behind them up to the railway station before coming back to the City Ground. I suppose it was quite apt because Nigel went on to play for Liverpool after leaving Forest. Needless to say, after that particular match both lads received a telling-off – and so did I because it was my son involved. But they both had their fish and chips afterwards and remained good pals.

Despite that little mishap, Brian trusted me enough to look after young Nigel and his older brother Simon during Forest's early trips to Wembley. Brian said to me, "You've got the most important job of the day – looking after my two bairns." I told him I was very proud to be given that responsibility. As a treat for the two boys, I went to one of Wembley's food kiosks to see if I could find something a bit different they might enjoy. I bought them both some chocolate-covered wagon wheels. It was the first time they had seen them and I'm pleased to say they went down very well indeed. I can still picture the excited looks on their faces, with their beaming smiles, as they tucked into their treats and a soft drink. In recent times, when I've reminded Nigel and Simon about those wagon wheels, it's still re-kindled some fond memories. After one of the Wembley games, I remember taking the pair round to the players' entrance so they could meet their Dad in the dressing room. They were delightful young lads, a pleasure to look after and I enjoyed their company.

Over the years, I was lucky enough to experience some tremendous trips to those famous twin towers, thanks to Brian. He would arrange tickets for the stadium and the car park. I would travel down there on a luxury coach that Michael Keeling organised for Brian's family and friends. Before the match, we would go to the Hilton Hotel on the Wembley complex and have a lovely meal on a table set-out for about 35 people. Afterwards, there would be a private room for us to have refreshments such as coffee and sandwiches. It was all done in style, whatever the result.

Having looked after young Nigel at Wembley when he was a boy, it was a privilege to watch him play there in later years. Brian used to refer to him as 'Our Nige' when we were talking privately and I know how proud he was to see Nigel not only play at Wembley but also win some England caps too. In the League Cup Final in 1989, Nigel scored twice as Forest beat Luton Town, despite going 1–0 down. Nigel scored a penalty to bring the score level. He must have felt immense pressure as he stepped-up to take that spot-kick. Neil Webb then put Forest ahead and Nigel scored again to make it 3–1. I don't recall any huge celebrations after that game, but it was significant for Brian. He had proved that he could produce a new, young and talented team without the help of Peter Taylor.

Playing for Forest and being not only the manager's son, but the son of Brian Clough, can't have been easy for Nigel. But he always conducted himself in a dignified manner and won the trust and respect of his teammates. 'The Number Nine,' as Brian referred to him at work, deserves a huge amount of credit for that. He had made his debut for Forest on Boxing Day 1984, in a 2–0 victory at home to Ipswich. Ironically, it was exactly twenty-two years after the fateful day that changed Brian's life. At Sunderland's Roker Park on Boxing Day 1962, Brian had suffered the injury which effectively ended his playing career. Fortunately, it would open the door to a whole new world of even greater success.

Following the Ipswich game, Nigel made a few more appearances for Forest that season and scored his first league goal for them in a 1–1 draw at home to Watford. He was playing alongside Garry Birtles, with whom he struck-up a great understanding and friendship. For the following four seasons, he was the Reds' top scorer. Nigel also established a superb understanding with Stuart Pearce. Many of Pearce's goals, besides those terrific free-kicks, were as a result of Nigel's passes. I watched in awe as Nigel would thread a pass through the narrowest of gaps in the opposition defence.

In the early days, Nigel would play for the Forest first team on a Saturday and then he would turn-out for the reserves in mid-week. I enjoyed watching him in the reserves – I think he had some of his best games for them. He would play sweeper and, despite his excellent goal-scoring record, I thought he was so good in that position that he should play there for the first XI. He would drop back a bit and not only win the ball, but keep it and then spray it about for his teammates with inch-perfect passes. I was fascinated to watch him play in that role and I would be really disappointed if he was substituted because, in my opinion, he was the star of the show. Thankfully, he would usually play the whole ninety minutes and he seemed to relish being there, even though it was the second-string side. You never got anything less than maximum effort from Nigel – the full measure.

I travelled all over the country watching the Forest reserves. Brian and I would sometimes travel in the car together, along with Michael Keeling. At other times we would be on the coach. After one game which the reserves lost, Brian asked me:

"What did you think to that then, Col?"

"It was brilliant," I said, having loved the whole experience.

"So you enjoyed it, did you?" Brian asked again.

"It was a great night, a brilliant game," I said.

Then came Brian's pointed reply: "Well, that's you finished, you won't be coming again."

I realised quickly I had said the wrong thing. Although he was joking about me not joining them for another game, he didn't like me saying I had enjoyed a good night when the team had lost. I'd got a bit carried away. To me, it did not matter they had lost, I had enjoyed it. But Brian hated losing.

He told me later: "You don't enjoy it when we lose – don't forget that."

We laughed about it, but I learned my lesson and didn't repeat the mistake the next time he asked me after a defeat.

"No, it was crap," was my reply.

Besides Nigel, the other player I waxed lyrical about, when Brian asked me, was Roy Keane. I saw him make his debut at Liverpool in August 1990. It was the first time I had seen him play. He had a fantastic game, even though Forest lost 2–0. It was a masterstroke of man-management by Brian because Roy didn't realise he was playing until the last minute. It meant there was no time for him to get nervous. In fact, I travelled up to Liverpool with Roy that day and neither of us had the faintest idea he would be making an appearance on the Anfield pitch. We thought he was going along just for the experience of it.

Roy had joined from the Irish side Cobh Ramblers and the trip to Liverpool was only the second game of the season. On the day of the match, Michael had driven me to Quarndon to pick up Brian at his house. While we were there, another car arrived and it was Brian's assistant Ron Fenton along with two players, including Roy. Brian gave him a glass of milk to drink – I think Roy was a bit reluctant at first, but he drank it. We then made our way up to Liverpool and I was in the same car as Ron and Roy. Ron was chatting away with me during the journey but I think Roy was fairly quiet and didn't say a lot. As it turned-out, he did all his talking on the pitch that night. He had only found out about an hour before kick-off that he was going to play. Although Forest lost, Roy described the whole experience as a dream come true. He was still a young, raw midfielder, but he was a great signing. And what a fantastic player he became, with such a presence on the pitch. I was not surprised to see him play at the highest level.

I think Roy's only regret about that impressive debut was that he didn't get the chance to tell his family in Ireland beforehand. But as time went by, Brian allowed him to return to visit his family whenever he could. Family values were so important to Brian. He loved Barbara and his children; he was always full of praise for them. He put his family on a pedestal. The players' families were important to him too and I got to meet a lot of them. When the young goalkeeper Chris Woods played in the 1978 League Cup Final, his Mum and Dad were with us at the Hilton Hotel. Another example came years later, when Nigel Jemson was brought into the side and his Mum and Dad were made welcome at the ground. His Mum used to love coming to the City Ground and she would be treated very well. Sometimes Brian reckoned Nigel Jemson was full of himself – he used to joke that Jemmo had as big a head as he did! But Brian knew how to the handle the young players and he soon brought them down to earth if he thought they were getting carried away. Of course, Jemson went on to score the winning goal in the 1990 League Cup Final. I always had a lot of time for him and thought he was a likeable lad.

You only have to look at the teams Brian developed in the late Eighties and around 1990 to see his expertise in dealing with young players. He had his own ways of making sure they were not getting into trouble away from the ground. In the case of Roy Keane, for example, I happened to tell Brian that I knew the landlady he was lodging with. My friend Tracey Gray was also the personnel manager where I worked at Pork Farms and lived in the West Bridgford area of Nottingham. When I told Brian he said: "That's good, I can keep an eye on him." Or words to that effect. A week or so later, Brian said to me: "Col, that friend of yours, does she like football?" When I said she probably did, he suggested that I bring her to a match, make sure she had a nice meal and then arrange for her to go into the guest room afterwards. So that's what I did and Tracey really enjoyed it. We were having a drink and talking to some of my friends after the game when Roy Keane suddenly walked in. It was highly unusual for a current player to walk into the guest room, but he had apparently been sent along to run an errand. When he saw Tracey, the look of surprise on his face was an absolute picture. We looked at each other and I could tell that he could not understand why his landlady was there. A few pleasantries were exchanged and then Roy went on his way. Afterwards, Brian thanked me. "We've got his card marked now," he said. It was simply Brian's way of letting Roy know that he had got an eye on him. Tracey told me that Roy was a perfect lodger. But even so, he knew that Brian would find out if he ever stepped out of line. In those days, he was just a young kid and he needed looking after.

But one thing was clear – whenever the young players were at the ground, Brian did not take too kindly to any interference from their families. My thoughts go back to his days at Derby and the right-back Ron Webster. I worked with Ron's Dad at the pit and we would often have a chat about the most recent game. He recalled how Ron had suffered an injury during a match. His Dad told me how, after the final whistle, he had knocked on the dressing room door to see how his lad was getting on. Brian gave him a right telling-off.

"You get off to your wife – I'll look after your son, he's my property while he's here," said Brian.

When I next saw Ron's Dad he told me: "On Monday morning there was the biggest bunch of flowers I've ever seen delivered to our house. They were especially for my wife. It was fantastic."

I thought that was a special touch from Brian and it was typical of him. He was very considerate, but it was his way of apologising too. He knew instinctively the right thing to do.

When one of his young players, who had come through the Forest ranks, wanted to leave, Brian asked me to have a quiet word with him to see if I could help change his mind. "You get on well with the lads, don't you Col?" he asked before adding, "You've got lads who work for you at the factory haven't you?" I said he was right on both counts. He then asked me to speak to a player who was looking to move to another club. "Will you have a word with him and point out that the grass isn't always greener?" I promised I'd do my best. The next time I saw the player, I took my opportunity to have a chat. He told me he was thinking of leaving Forest to develop his career.

I talked to him as a friend – a friend who was quite a bit older – but I didn't let on that Brian had asked me to have a word. I told him: "No matter what walk of life you're in, there'll always be opportunities and it's not easy to turn them down. But you really should think about what it's like here at Forest and whether it's worth the move. In my situation, I wouldn't move for £100, for example, but if I was offered £50,000 then I couldn't refuse it. But if I'm happy where I am, and it's only a question of a few quid, there is no way that I would leave. Especially when you know the area and the people. You like living round here, don't you?" He told me he loved living in the area. Our chat continued and we ended-up talking for quite a while, but despite my best efforts, he decided to leave. Brian thanked me for trying; he really didn't want him to go.

Another player I used to chat to was the midfielder, Steve Hodge. I thought he was a lovely young man and I enjoyed his company. Sometimes he would come into the City Ground guest room after a match and I would get on well with him. Whenever I was staying overnight in the team hotel for an away game, Steve would often join me and Albert the driver for breakfast and we would have a good chat. But on one trip, we had arrived at the hotel and Steve was injured. Brian said Steve should get himself home and I was asked to help him find his way back to the motorway. He followed me in convoy until he knew which road to take.

Although I've spoken here about some of the young players, Brian knew how to get the best out of all the members of his team, whatever their age. From what I've heard, some needed an arm around the shoulder and regular praise, while others required the proverbial boot up the backside. He could soon bring them down a peg or two if he thought they were getting carried away. His one-liners were priceless. I heard that one player, who had been dropped to the second team, asked him why. The explanation was simple: "Because we haven't got a third team."

A few of the players have now gone on to have careers in management themselves. And having worked for the master manager, it can only have served to benefit them. I'm very pleased to see Nigel establish himself as a manager in his own right. But I was absolutely gutted when he was sacked from Derby County in 2013 after more than four years in charge. I could not see any justification for him to lose his job, considering the team he was building and the fact he did not have a lot of money to work with. He had remained loyal to Derby through thick and thin and the whole thing left a sour taste for me. Brian always preached loyalty and now I'm pleased to say that same quality is in evidence at Sheffield United, where Nigel has taken the likes of John Brayford to play for him. Brayford had played for him at Derby and when I watched him have such a crucial role in United's FA Cup victory over Fulham, I couldn't help but think of that word: loyalty.

Even in the short time that Nigel has been at Bramall Lane, I can see his style of football shining through. I'm delighted he took the job there; it is important continuity for him. I have no doubt at all that his Dad would have approved of the decision to take the job and for him to get back into management at the earliest opportunity. And that brings to mind an occasion when Brian addressed the gathered media at an event – and he was asked about Nigel.

"He's a man in his own right and he can cope," said Brian. "He's been playing football for a long, long time – have you met him?"

Silence from the press pack.

"No?" asked Brian, before he continued: "Well, you should meet him and you'll see some of the good sides of the game. Instead of reading about someone who kicks a taxi or gets thrown out of a club or anything like that. So if you get the chance, say hello to him."

Brave member of the press pack: "He doesn't talk to us, Brian."

Brian: "Well, to be fair, my instant reply to that is – he's a good judge."
Cue laughter.

5.

TV Times

Picture the scene. Brian walks into the chairman's office; with a player he is about to sign. "Good morning, Brian. Contracts are drawn up and ready for signature," says the chairman. "Pop your signature on there, young man," says Brian and the player attempts to sign using an ordinary ball-point pen. The chairman snatches the pen disapprovingly and replaces it with his own.

"Come, come," says the chairman. "You aren't at City now. This is a club with prestige, my boy. A club with heritage. I think a Parker Harlequin is more appropriate."

As you may have guessed, this was not an ordinary signing session for a new player. Brian was starring in an advert for Parker pens and the script had been carefully written. We had travelled down to Arsenal's Highbury Stadium for the filming of the advert, which was set in the chairman's office. It was such a privilege to watch Brian at work in that situation. The actor Arthur Lowe took the role of the chairman – he was famous for playing Captain Mainwaring in *Dad's Army* and was an absolute gentleman in real life too.

It was almost a full day of filming and the staff at Highbury looked after us all really well, keeping us supplied with refreshments. I saw quite a few of the Arsenal players and there was a bit of banter with them. "Tell Brian I want to play for him," one of them shouted, while another called over "Tell Brian I want a contract too." Brian had asked that Peter Taylor should make an appearance in the advert and Peter was filmed sitting in the outer office reading a copy of the Sporting Life. During a break in filming, Peter persuaded me to ask Arthur Lowe if he would like a cup of tea. I got on well with Peter who was a born comedian. Sometimes he liked to put me in these unusual situations and then watch to see how I got out of them. I was a bit apprehensive about approaching Mr Lowe because he was such a famous actor, so I walked up to his wife first. She had been playing the role of the chairman's secretary in the advert and I asked her: "Do you think Mr Lowe would like a drink?" She said they had just flown in from Australia so he was very tired and that I should go and ask him. He was dressed immaculately in a suit, a very imposing figure. Taking a deep breath, I decided to approach him.

"Mr Lowe?" I began, nervously.

"Yes, dear boy," he replied and for a moment I felt like young Private Pike in *Dad's Army*.

"I wondered if you would like a cup of tea?" I enquired, knowing Peter would be watching my every move at this point

"Oh yes, that would be a very good idea, thank you so much."

I was so pleased with myself – I was getting a cup of tea for the famous Captain Mainwaring. And unlike Corporal Jones, I didn't panic about it! (Sorry about that, but I couldn't resist).

When the filming continued, Brian looked at the player as the new signing held the pen.

"A fine ball pen, for a fine ball player," was Brian's next line. I still have the original script for the advert, which describes both the dialogue and the directions for the actors and film crew. In it, Arthur Lowe has a comic line at Brian's expense. Speaking about the new player and the pen he adds: "Aye, we'll be happy if you perform as well. Glides beautifully across the surface. Runs fluently for four miles without stopping, and isn't temperamental like some I could mention," at which point he gives Brian a sideways glance. As I said, it was a well-written script. The advert was very successful and had a good long run on television.

Brian loved the opportunities to do a bit of acting in front of the television cameras. He was a great performer and completely in his element. For another advert, promoting East Midlands Electricity, we travelled to London again. It was for the company's Economy Seven tariff and various sets had been built for them to film in. The main set was the kitchen. Brian was working with the lovely actress Cherie Lunghi. After shooting various scenes, the producer was clearly impressed with the football manager-turned-actor. "He's a natural," he said. But it also meant they had a problem. Most of the filming was completed quite quickly, but the studio and crew had been booked for the whole day. I think they ended-up having to pad it out and film some of the scenes two or three times, even though they had been happy with the first take.

When Brian was asked to make a cameo appearance in the television series *Boon*, starring Michael Elphick, the filming took place a little nearer to home. I got a phone call from Michael Keeling who asked me to meet them. "We've got to go to a pub in Beeston – I've no idea where it is," he said. I knew where Beeston was, on the outskirts of Nottingham, so I met Michael and Brian and once again became 'The Navigator,' directing them to the pub where the filming would take place. When we arrived, Brian double-checked with me that it was definitely the right venue and Michael parked the car nearby. Brian sent Michael and me into the pub first and we spoke to the producers, who explained what would be happening. Not surprisingly, they wanted to know where Brian was. A little while later, Brian walked in. He had kept them waiting – it was just a little reminder that he was the boss. The episode was called 'Work, Rest and Play' and featured the actor John Hannah as a Scottish footballer called Willie Connolly who was dealing with a dodgy agent. Just as Willie was about to sign on the dotted line in the pub, Brian walked in to rescue the situation and saved

Willie from entering into a deal which would have cost him a great deal financially. "Be careful you've read the small print, young man," was Brian's first line.

But there were no lines to learn when Brian appeared on the Parkinson chat show. Although it was a straightforward interview for him, it was an unforgettable experience for me. I was sitting in the hospitality suite with Brian, Peter, Michael and another friend, Mike Dickinson. Michael Parkinson came in and said he needed to take Brian to the make-up department to get ready for the show. We all had a bit of a joke about Brian needing make-up and then Michael Parkinson asked if a couple of us would go into the main studio for a rehearsal, to test the cameras and the music. Mike Dickinson and I volunteered and within a few minutes we were both walking down the famous Parkinson steps, with the theme tune playing, as if we were guests about to be interviewed. The warm-up man, who had been telling jokes to the audience to get them ready for the show, pretended to be Michael Parkinson and ushered us to the seats, opposite the one to be occupied by 'Parky'. The technical staff said everything appeared to be working well and we made our way back to the hospitality suite, where a buffet was laid-out.

Peter Taylor said: "Col, can you check out that pork pie for us?" I went over to the table to see what it was like. One of the other guests, Warren Mitchell (who played the character Alf Garnett) watched me and asked: "What's he doing that for?"

Peter replied: "Colin works for the company which makes the best pork pies in England. He'll tell us whether they are any good or not."

"Well, it won't bother me," came the reply. "I don't eat pork."

As we started chatting, someone asked Mr Mitchell about supporting West Ham. He said he wasn't a Hammers supporter – "only on television." Although Alf Garnett was a West Ham man, Mr Mitchell said he supported Chelsea. He then gave us ten minutes as that famous comic character and it was absolutely hilarious. I think he was warming himself up before going on television. I got the impression that he was a very private person away from the cameras. He was very eloquent, despite the image of his loud-mouthed alter ego. I met him again some months later when I was at Stamford Bridge to watch Forest play Chelsea. I mentioned the Parkinson show and the pork pies and we had a good conversation.

The trip to see Brian interviewed by Michael Parkinson was certainly an entertaining one. They had known each other for years and both loved cricket. One of the subjects they talked about was playing cricket for the Lord's Taverners. Brian told me that when he played in those charity matches, the bowlers would deliver the ball really aggressively at him because he was famous. "I'm only going there to give them support and I'm wondering where the ball is going to hit me," he told me. "Not only do they want to *bowl* me out – they want to *knock* me out!"

On many occasions, I would travel with Brian for his personal appearances, interviews and filming for television. He particularly enjoyed question-and-answer sessions with fans, but if anyone questioned his methods or decisions (if they were brave enough to do so), they would soon get short shrift. He was as sharp as a tack and quickly had an answer for them. After all, Brian's record spoke for itself, so he didn't stand for any criticism of the way he did things if any supporter put their head in the lion's den and questioned his methods. He loved holding court and giving his opinions, not just on football but anything you wanted to discuss, politics for example. In private moments, Brian and I would discuss politics together, both being Labour supporters. We would try to put the world to rights and Brian would know that he was gently winding-up our friend Michael who was a Conservative. But it was all gentle banter and it got us through many long miles travelling together in the car.

One of Brian's great friends from the world of television was the commentator, Brian Moore. They worked together a lot over the years and

Brian (Clough) always had a great deal of admiration for him. Brian would comment on how well he thought his friend commentated and presented programmes, compared with many others in the industry. "Just listen to all the rubbish these days," Brian would tell me. "They tell you everything. From who the man on the gate is, to what his grandmother's name is and how many cups of tea he's drunk. It's all too much, it's ridiculous."

When Sky TV came on the scene, Brian said: "Col, you'll be watching football on a Sunday teatime. You'll be so saturated with it, you won't like it." And he's right. I don't. Too much football on television can dilute the entertainment value if you're not careful. I still like watching Arsenal when their games are shown on TV – Brian was full of praise for the Gunners and their manager, Arsene Wenger, when they eventually beat Nottingham Forest's record of forty-two games unbeaten. I enjoy watching their style of play and I can understand why Brian admired them. I like to watch Manchester City too. But I get fed-up with many of the people who associate themselves with Manchester United. You see them wearing Man Utd shirts in the street, yet they've never been to Old Trafford and probably hardly ever watched them on television either.

As far as Brian was concerned, the way his mate Brian Moore conducted himself was exactly how football presentation should be carried out on the television. They were such good friends that Brian Moore was invited to a birthday party for Brian's wife, Barbara. It was at a hotel in Derbyshire and my wife Irene and I sat alongside the presenter and his wife. I discovered that we shared a passion for collecting porcelain and Brian (Moore) told me how he loved the Derbyshire Dales and liked the Staffordshire pottery trail, where you could visit various places to buy pots and plates. On his recommendation, I later went on the trail and remember going down lots of little side streets among the potteries. You could look inside the lovely old buildings and search through boxes full of straw to uncover some very collectable items. The two Brian's would always keep in touch whenever they could. If Forest were playing on the south coast, Brian Moore would try to join us for a meal at a hotel in Brighton, either the night before the game or at lunchtime.

When we learned the news, in 2001, that Brian Moore had passed away, it was obviously a very sad day and there were many tributes from leading names in the world of football. I was struggling with my own health around that time, so Brian arranged for us to be driven to the funeral. At the service, I sat next to Sir Trevor Brooking. It was a day to remember all the good times and celebrate Brian Moore's life. One of the memorable and amusing TV appearances featuring the two Brian's happened during the 1986 World Cup when the former England striker Mick Channon was also with them in the studio. I think Mick was talking about the strength of the other sides, compared to England. He said: "The Irish have done it, the French do it, the West Germans do it..." Then Brian picked-up: "Even educated fleas do it." Smiles and laughter all round, including a chuckle from the presenter. Perfect.

6.

Bring Me Sunshine

If anyone had recognised Brian, they wouldn't have believed it. There he was, walking alongside me, carrying a big bag of laundry along the seafront in Majorca. It was a regular task for us, taking the laundry from Brian's apartment in the resort of Cala Millor to a little launderette nearby for it to be washed and returned. He knew that the laundry could be collected from the apartment if he had wanted that, but he insisted on taking it himself and would always ask me to join him. "This is mine and Col's job," he would tell his family. So that's what happened: the most charismatic football manager in the world was carrying bags of dirty washing along the side streets and the seafront. And all in the lovely morning sunshine. He loved it.

Once we had delivered the laundry, we would be tired out because the bags were heavy and the weather was red-hot. So our routine was to then find a little cafe tucked away where there would be no other British people or holidaymakers. We would sit and have a chat and enjoy a small cold drink to cool down. We would talk about things in general; nothing to do with football – after all, Brian was on holiday. I felt so comfortable in Brian's company that, to me, it felt like two blokes having a chat. He would often ask about my job and how it was going. I was in charge of an engineering department at Pork Farms and if I had a problem with someone at work I would talk to Brian about it. Sometimes he would suggest that I should stop the wages of someone if I thought they weren't doing their job properly. "You can't do that in my line of work," I'd tell him. "Well, you can in my game," he'd reply. "Well, I just can't do it Brian, it doesn't work like that." He could not understand that it was impossible for me to immediately withhold someone's wages because their work was not up to scratch. The firm I worked for had set procedures that would have to be followed, if I thought they were necessary. Brian ran his football club from top to bottom so my working environment was a different world to the one he knew inside out.

We would sit near the front of the cafe so we could look down the street. He was usually very welcoming to people who approached him and would sign autographs and have a chat with them. But sometimes when a crowd of holidaymakers walked by, he would say to me "Right, sit back, Col," so we wouldn't be seen and we could continue our private conversation. On one occasion he said: "Hey Col, I think you might fancy this young lady who's coming towards us." It was my wife, Irene. She stayed talking to us for a little while and then went shopping. After a few minutes, Brian's attention was grabbed by a little barber's shop across the road. He had been fascinated watching the people going in and out of the tiny shop.

"I'm going to get my hair cut," he suddenly declared. I'm not sure whether his hair needed cutting, but he was intrigued by this little shop – and now there was no stopping him.

"Well, I'll wait here for you," I told him.

"No, you come with me," Brian insisted, so I did.

Brian couldn't speak Spanish, but he sat down in the chair and they put the gown around him. It was a business run by a father and son partnership and they were both impeccably turned-out. Brian was given a shave, using the foam and a cut-throat razor, and then had his hair cut. The barber kept asking him things and pointing. He was interested to know whether Brian wanted any hair-gel or things like that, and Brian kept nodding. "Yes, I'll have that ... and that ... and that," he said, thoroughly enjoying the whole experience. Brian had the complete works that morning: hot towels, tints, gels and creams. You name it, he had it. Before Brian had walked into the shop, he had had a good head of hair, but by the time it was over the barber had virtually given him a crew cut. When they took the gown away and he stood up, it was hard to recognise him. Although his new look came as a bit of a shock at the time, I suppose he was only following the orders he gave to some of his team – get that hair cut!

Cala Millor was a favourite holiday destination for Brian. Sometimes he would take his players there for a pre-season or mid-season break, at other times it would be only his family and friends who would be invited. I was very fortunate to be invited both with the team and as part of a private group consisting of his family and close-knit circle of friends. When the team was with us, he would insist that any injured players should have a walk in the sea. I think he believed it would have some healing proper-ties for them. We would be walking together down the beach and he'd say: "Right you lot, get in that sea and get your legs right!" He had originally done something similar with the Hartlepool players at Runswick Bay, although the North Sea off the north-east coast of England was probably much colder!

Whenever I stayed in Cala Millor, it felt like I was part of one big, happy family. Sometimes there would be a group of 12 or 14 of us and we would almost take-over a whole restaurant. A bar called The Shack, with a bamboo front, was a focal point for the players. They would be given quite a bit freedom to enjoy themselves, within reason. Brian felt that rest and relaxation was vital for the players. The sunshine did them good and it was a great bonding exercise too, to maintain that healthy team spirit. The Forest players went there shortly before winning the European Cup for a second time. It had been a long, hard season and Brian felt that a break in the sunshine was just what they needed. Once again, it was a fantastic piece of management. Even after the days of European Cup success, he continued to take his teams and backroom staff to Cala Millor.

Sometimes the Forest team would play a match against a local Spanish club. But there was one game in particular that could not be described as 'friendly.' Forest had prepared in their usual relaxed style. In fact, they had taken an 'extra man' with them on the team bus – he ran a little beach-bar and the players had met him while having a kick-about on the sand. So Brian decided they would take him with them. They even gave him a track-suit and let him warm-up with them on the pitch before kick-off. But once the game was underway, the mood changed very quickly. The local Spanish side went hell for leather, kicking the Forest players off the park. It became quite dangerous for them. They had gone to Majorca for a relaxing break ahead of a big match at home a few days later, so they did not expect to face such rough treatment. Brian was remonstrating to the referee about the heavy-duty tackling, but the ref simply sent him off. Brian wouldn't go and in the end a policeman had to escort him down the tunnel. A few minutes later he re-emerged wearing a cap and scarf to disguise himself and sat near the back of the dug-out. Brian and the entire team were relieved when the final whistle was blown.

Most Sundays when we were in Cala Millor we would take a trip up to the nearby town of Son Servera, which is rich in history. Brian would arrange a couple of taxis for his family and friends and we would then sit in the town square and enjoy the surroundings. His good friend and former Forest chairman, Stuart Dryden, was a Catholic and he and Brian would often go to the church service while we were there. It would always be a very relaxing day before heading back to where we were staying.

Talking of relaxation, Brian, like many of us, also enjoyed reading a good book while on holiday. Sometimes he would have a quiet hour or two by himself, engrossed in a book. At other times we would all sit together as a group of friends and each have a book or magazine. On one occasion he spotted that I was reading a book I had taken with me about the Midland Railway in Derbyshire. As an engineer, I was very interested in the story of this railway and how a tunnel had been built into the land at Clay Cross. "What have you got there, Col?" Brian asked me. I explained what the book was about and he asked if he could have a look at it. After flicking through some of the pages, he said he would like to borrow it when I had finished. So I lent him the paperback and he became fascinated by the story of social history that it told. When he handed it back to me, he described it as one of the best books he had ever read.

*   *   *

Watching Forest play abroad was always a fantastic experience, thanks to Brian. When we flew anywhere, it was usually in style. The hotels that we stayed in were superb. Local dignitaries, like the Mayor, would go to the team hotel to meet Brian and the players. Brian told me that he was keen to get the players interested in going out and looking round these new places, experiencing different cultures and seeing the local sights. He admitted that, as a player himself, he had been the worst for missing out on things like that. When he had been to Canada as part of a team, the bus had stopped at Niagra Falls. "Can you guess what I did?" Brian asked me. Before I could answer, he added: "I stayed on the bus, playing cards! I think to myself 'what a waste that was.' That's why I want them (the players) to go out and do things."

Some of the trips for the European Cup games were incredible. Although many people will remember the two finals, with Forest achieving the amazing feat of winning the trophy twice in consecutive years, the matches, which will always standout for me, were the semi-finals. In those days, only teams that had won their league title could enter the competition. There was no league; it was simply each country's champions competing in a knockout competition played over two legs in each round, before the best reached the final. In 1979, Forest faced Cologne in the semi-final, having beaten Liverpool, AEK Athens and Grasshoppers of Zurich.

The first-leg of the match against Cologne must go down as one of the City Ground classics. In fact, it was one of the epic tussles of European football. I was one of nearly 41,000 spectators who watched in shock as the Germans attacked from the start and soon found themselves two goals up, silencing the home fans. The pitch was a complete mud bath but the visitors quickly got to grips with the conditions. Many teams may have crumbled under the pressure, but it was fantastic to see Forest fight back. A header by Garry Birtles brought the Reds back into the game, but as Forest pushed for an equaliser the Germans found space at the other end and nearly made it 3–1. It was a very nervous half-time break. I remember thinking what a tough task Brian was facing, especially as Cologne had two away goals, which would count double if the score over the two legs was even.

The relief around the City Ground when Ian Bowyer scored the equaliser was immense. He had been pushed into midfield when Archie Gemmill went off injured. 'Bomber' Bowyer hit a low right-foot drive through a crowded penalty box to bring the score level. The stadium erupted when John Robertson flung himself forward to give Forest a 3–2 lead with a rare header. We thought that was it: Forest had a precious lead to take to Germany two weeks later. But the visitors had other plans and caught the Reds on the break with an equaliser from their Japanese substitute, Yasuhiko Okudera. Forest now needed a win in the second-leg or a high-scoring draw (something like 4–4) to reach the Final.

But Brian was convinced that his team had the quality to win. He told the media: "I hope that no one is stupid enough to write us off." Yes, many people had written Forest off, but that didn't stop us enjoying the trip to Cologne and a memorable match. I was part of the VIP party (family, friends and directors), which flew from East Midlands Airport for the game. We were treated so well from the moment we arrived at our local airport, with a private room being provided for us. Our hotel was in the centre of Cologne, near the cathedral. When we arrived in Germany, the confidence of our hosts was clear to see. There were even posters advertising how to buy tickets for the final! They made the mistake of counting their chickens, as they say.

Viv Anderson and Kenny Burns, who had been unable to play in the first-leg, returned for the away match in front of 60,000 people in the huge Muengersdorf Stadium. Forest's orders were straightforward. If they could keep a clean sheet, the vital goal might just arrive. Although the home side was soon on the attack, Forest dealt well with the early pressure and the score was goalless at half-time. In the second half, Forest won a corner on the left, which was taken by the ever-dependable John Robertson. He floated the ball to the near post where the excellent Birtles flicked a header backwards and Ian Bowyer stooped to nod the ball into the net. It was probably the most important goal that 'Bomber' had ever scored. The under-dogs were through to the Final, even though the match against Cologne had seemed like a final itself. It had been such an uphill battle for Forest. In some ways, the Final in Munich was almost an anti-climax because Cologne had been the favourites and no one had really heard of Forest's opponents, Malmo of Sweden. Brian described it as a 'Cinderella' Final because two of the smaller clubs in the competition had got through despite the challenges of the more established teams. For Forest to win the European Cup was like being in dreamland and they deserved it. Not only that, but they did it again the following year after another classic semi-final against Ajax of Amsterdam.

The first-leg match against Ajax at the City Ground was a tremendous spectacle. The visitors came with an amazing pedigree of having won the European Cup in three consecutive seasons in the early Seventies. They had also scored some thirty goals on their way to reaching the semi-final that season. But Brian would not let his team be intimidated by that kind of record and Forest pushed forward from the kick-off, producing the kind of opportunities that were sure to lead to goals. The breakthrough came just after half an hour when Trevor Francis drove the ball into the net at close-range following a John Robertson corner. Ajax, who had been free scoring in the earlier rounds of the competition, found themselves pinned back and relying heavily on their defence. It was great to see Forest take the game to them and the further pressure paid off in the second half when one of their players handled the ball and Robertson scored from the resulting penalty. Forest won the game 2–0, with Brian describing it as a superb performance. But he admitted he would have preferred a third goal, which would surely have killed the tie altogether.

In the return leg in Amsterdam, you could clearly see why Brian had hoped for goal number three at the City Ground. Ajax produced wave after wave of attacks in front of their excited and very noisy fans. Due to the demand for tickets, the home side had changed the venue from their own ground to the much larger Olympic Stadium, with around 60,000 spectators. Forest defended magnificently but could not hold on to a clean sheet. Soren Lerby scored in the second half with a header and his team rushed back to the centre circle to get the game restarted. Although Forest lost the game 1–0, they qualified for the Final 2–1 on aggregate. I was lucky enough to fly back with the team on that occasion. At the airport, before the journey home, some of the players went shopping and Brian began to get frantic because they were taking so long and the flight-time was approaching. I managed to find some of the players and urged them to hurry up. The plane itself was a bit of a tin bucket, but we didn't mind. As it taxied on the runway before take-off, the players started singing 'Here we go, here we go ...' in chorus. It was a fantastic atmosphere and a real privilege to be part of it all. I thought to myself, 'I'm with the European Champions – what could be better than this?' Of course, a little over a month later things did get better, when the team won the European Cup for a second time. That Cala Millor sunshine had worked wonders once again.

*   *   *

Cala Millor was not the only sunshine destination for us. I joined Brian and the Forest team for a mid-season break to the resort of Magaluf, which is also on the island of Majorca. The former Liverpool player John Toshack was there and he would join us every day and talk to Brian. He seemed a very eloquent man and they appeared to get on well. During our break there, a few of us had a good card school going, although Brian wasn't involved. Michael Keeling and I were doing really well against some of the others. But then we started to feel the worse for wear and began losing. Michael decided to go back to the hotel on his own and shortly afterwards I felt it was time to call it a day too. But it began pouring with rain and I stood in a doorway with one of the Forest players as we looked at the rain lashing down. He challenged me to a race back to the hotel. So we set-off running and got soaking wet. Even so, I beat him back to the hotel. "I didn't know you could run so fast," he told me. I joked that it must have been due to whatever had been put in my drinks that evening. Not surprisingly, the next morning Michael and I had huge hangovers.

There were also several trips to Torremolinos on the Costa Del Sol in southern Spain. It was the favourite holiday destination of the trainer, Jimmy Gordon. But unfortunately Jimmy could not be there for one of our visits, so we had a special cake made and brought it back for him. It was a special occasion and Jimmy was absolutely delighted, even though he did not usually show much emotion in public. We also presented him with a basket of goodies including different kinds of fruit and a bottle of champagne, even though he didn't drink!

The businessman Sir Fred Pontin, who founded the famous holiday camp chain, had two hotels in Torremolinos and he always enjoyed it when Forest came to visit. During one particular trip, we had some of the 'walking wounded' with us such as Frank Clark and Ian Bowyer who were recovering from injuries. We were all trying to listen to a radio to find-out the result of a crucial Forest match back home. Several of the players' wives were there too and Sir Fred arranged a wonderful buffet for us and made sure he said hello to everyone. Sir Fred was a true pioneer who had left school at 15 without any qualifications and went on to build an impressive holiday empire from scratch. In a way, you could say his rise to success from very humble beginnings mirrored those of Brian's. Sir Fred died in October 2000 after suffering a stroke at the grand age of 93. A friend of his is quoted as saying: "He was in good spirits to the end ... he simply ran out of breath."

During the mid-1980's, Brian agreed to take the Forest team for a winter trip to Malta. I was invited along too and straight after a match in England we all made our way to the airport for the flight to the lovely Mediterranean island. We were guests of the Maltese Government and they arranged special receptions and presentations for us. We signed their guest book and I noticed that on another page were the signatures of Queen Elizabeth and Prince Philip from a previous visit. I was proud that 'Nottingham Forest' and my own name were added to that special book. Our hosts took us to the island of Gozo on one of their Naval ships. The captain heard that I had been in the Royal Navy and allowed me to steer the ship. I turned to Brian and said: "This is fabulous, isn't it?"

"Fabulous?" he replied, "I can't wait to get off this ship – I hate ships!"

"Don't worry, Brian," I said, trying to cheer him up. "I'm steering it – we'll be OK."

I've still got a photo of Brian standing on the ship while it was sailing. He has his arms folded and doesn't look very happy about the whole experience. When we returned to the hotel that night we played snooker and I took-on the Forest secretary, Ken Smales, who was usually unbeatable at that game. To everyone's surprise I won – and it boosted my reputation considerably.

Forest played the inaugural game at a stadium in Malta's capital, Valletta. When we arrived at the stadium we sat in the Directors' Box. Brian said: "Col, you come and sit with me." So, there we were, sitting in the box – with the President of Malta sitting directly in front of us. But on the way to the stadium we had noticed a lot of protests and people with placards – there was quite a lot of civil unrest that day. I turned to Brian and said: "I'm not happy sitting just here." He replied: "Why? What's the matter with you?" I told him: "If anyone decides to assassinate the President, and they miss, they're going to hit either you or me." Brian replied: "Hey, you're spot on. Come on, let's move." Thankfully there was no attempt on the President's life, but we felt we had done the right thing in the circumstances.

I was invited to an official banquet while we were there and it was held in very palatial surroundings. Brian didn't attend that event, so when it was time for the presentations I received the gifts on behalf of our party. I was absolutely delighted when Brian insisted that I keep one of the gifts as a momento of the visit: a little box with a silver Maltese cross inside.

There was also a trip to a restaurant which belonged to the Maltese international centre-half. One of the topics of conversation during that meal was Roy McFarland – because he and the Maltese player were friends. It was a big group of us – about 28 in total – and as we sat at the table all the menus were handed-out. Then suddenly Brian halted the proceedings:

"Right, you can put all the menus away," he declared. "I know what we're all having. It's pizzas for everybody."

Brian didn't want any fuss on that occasion. I don't think he was particularly fond of pizza, but he said: "That poor waiter, going around all these people taking orders for this and orders for that. I'll make it easy for him – everyone's having pizza." It was a very enjoyable meal and there is a lovely photo of a group of us on the restaurant balcony, with Brian waving.

When we returned to England, Michael and I drove straight back to Nottingham with a couple of the players who had picked-up injuries and needed treatment. But a short time later I also drove into a spot of bother at my place of work. Although I was a senior manager at the Pork Farms factory, in charge of the engineering department, I hadn't got permission from my boss to go on the Malta trip and I almost got the sack as a result. Working in the food industry, Christmas was always a critical time and I should have been there in the lead-up to the festive period. It was stupid of me to have gone away when I did. I got on well with my boss, Brian Stein, but I had pushed the boundaries too far on that occasion. He called me into his office and I feared the worst. I explained that I was sorry but the invitation had been too good to miss. The boss gave me a warning and I kept my job. He could have taken much more severe action against me and fortunately it did not affect our friendship.

Looking back at all the trips I was invited on, all the matches I went to (often leaving the office just after lunchtime for away games) and the host of TV and radio appearances when I accompanied Brian, it is easy to wonder how I kept a full-time job at the same time. I have to say that my employers were always brilliant at letting me have the time off to pursue all these things. They were usually very flexible and there was a lot of give-and-take, which I appreciated. I received four weeks holiday a year because I was a senior manager and I also worked most of the Bank Holidays. I decided to take my annual holiday in fragments, two days here and two days there, and my boss said he preferred it that way. It suited the company to have me working four days in a particular week rather than taking a three-week block as a holiday.

I also got into the boss' good books by arranging for him and other company managers to sit in the Directors' Box. I introduced Brian Stein to the other significant Brian in my life and the three of us played cards and dominoes together. So whenever I needed a couple of days off to join Brian (Clough) or Forest, for whatever reason, I had that understanding and flexibility from my employers. Excluding the episode over the Malta trip, I never neglected my job. In fact I worked extremely hard for the firm, produced quite a few innovations and helped them make a lot of money. I also had a very good deputy, which was a big help in certain situations. I don't think the flexible working arrangement would have panned-out so well at any other company, so I was very lucky.

There is one other foreign trip I must mention because it was a real eye-opener. In September 1983 we travelled to East Germany to play Vorwaerts, a club on the German-Polish border, in the first round of the UEFA Cup. It was behind the Iron Curtain in those days and we stayed in Berlin (behind the infamous wall). We travelled by bus to the game in Frankfurt (Oder) and there were special security police officers looking after us – and no doubt keeping a suspicious eye on us too! The night of the match was bitterly cold. In fact it was so cold it was hard to concentrate on watching the game. Forest won 1–0, thanks to an Ian Bowyer goal, having won the first leg at home 2–0. There was a security man following us wherever we went and after a while it became annoying. Compared to the surroundings, the hotel we stayed in felt like a cocoon, a haven of opulent tranquility. As soon as you walked outside, it was all very different. It was like walking back into the 1930s. The shops were barren and there were ruined buildings all over the place. People would be asking us to sell them any spare clothes we had. They wanted anything – trousers, shirts and coats. I heard that during a sight-seeing trip, the tour guide – thinking he had completed his duties – asked if there was anything else he could do. "Yes there is," said Brian. "You can knock down that wall for a start."

7.

Food Glorious Food

Getting to know Brian didn't just open my eyes to a world of fantastic opportunities and a valued friendship, it also introduced me to a whole new world of food! He encouraged me to try all kinds of weird and wonderful dishes. Before I met Brian I was very unadventurous when it came to trying different types of food. But that soon changed.

At a restaurant in Cala Millor, Brian ordered a big bowl of unusual-looking food, which turned out to be a local delicacy. It consisted of a liquid with little squids and octopuses floating in it. Brian said: "Hey Col, you should have some of this." The look on my face couldn't hide my reluctance.

"What's the matter?" he asked.

"I don't like it, Brian."

"Well, you've never tried it. Come on, try this."

So I tried a mouthful and ended-up with little tentacles hanging out of my mouth. I managed to swallow it all and Brian asked if I would like some more.

"It was alright, wasn't it Col?" he asked, encouragingly.

"Yes, not bad Brian," I said, hoping that would be my last taste of this unusual dish.

"Well, have some more."

"No thanks, Brian. That's quite sufficient for me." I think he got the message.

When we were on holiday, Brian would have a go at eating anything. Nothing phased him. These days, I think he would have been a star of the Bush Tucker Trial on the television jungle challenge 'I'm A Celebrity...' During our visits to the town of Son Servera, he would order all kinds of things, like tripe, suckling pig and pigs' trotters. I think his taste buds had developed quite a bit since his days as a young player, when he went to Russia with the England Under-23 squad and was faced with a bowl of consommé soup with a raw egg in it. At that time, I think he would have been fine with just a bowl of soup, but the fact it had a raw egg in it as well – looking up at him "like a single eye" – made it quite a challenge to eat. Before going on that England trip, he was grateful for the advice of Bobby Charlton who had warned him about the food – and suggested he take plenty of chocolate with him.

There was more unusual soup on the menu when we were on the beach in Majorca. The Forest players had been having a little kick-about on the sand with some of the local waiters. It was winter and we bought some food from a beachside bar. The players were so hungry that they virtually bought all the food available – the little man who ran the bar must have thought all his Christmases had come at once. Brian bought some gezpacho – a tomato-based vegetable soup, served cold. He insisted that we all drank this soup, even though we were absolutely freezing. "Hey, are you enjoying your soup, lads?" he shouted. "Oh, yes, Brian," I replied. "It's fabulous." Who was I kidding?

I also had an experience with an oyster, which I will never forget. We were staying on the south coast for a Forest match and Brian's friend, the commentator Brian Moore, joined us for a meal. We were having a drink beforehand when a dish of oysters appeared. Brian (Clough) asked if I liked oysters and I had to be honest and say that I had never tried them. "Well, have one of these," he said, handing me the plate. I had seen other people eat them and they seemed to enjoy them, so I thought it would be a good idea to give them a try. I was a bit apprehensive, but I thought that if I could master the art of eating them, it would be a good thing. Here was my chance. I picked-up one of the oysters and popped it in my mouth. But then I suddenly began to wish I hadn't. Brian had recommended that I just swallow it, rather than bite it. But I just couldn't bring myself to swallow it. It just wouldn't go down. The two Brian's continued talking and I kept trying to swallow the wretched thing, but to no avail. I began to feel really uncomfortable. When they weren't looking, I grabbed a napkin, spat out the oyster and put it in my pocket. I daren't tell Brian that I didn't like it; he thought that I'd eaten it. He asked me what I thought. "Oh, it was good, Brian, very good," I smiled, putting on a brave face. Then came the offer of another one. "Oh, no I'm fine thanks," I said, "One's enough for me." Little did he know the full truth of my reply. I didn't know what to do with the troublesome oyster in my pocket, as there was no immediate opportunity to ensure its safe disposal, so it stayed in my pocket for about two hours!

I felt much more comfortable sharing a Chinese takeaway with Brian. There were times we would eat at his house and Brian would place an order with the local Chinese takeaway called Shing Do. I remember Nigel went to collect one of the meals and returned with lots of different packets containing all kinds of wonderful Chinese food. We sat in Brian's lounge and it was all very relaxed as we savoured the different flavours, eating the various dishes on trays on our laps. But it wasn't just Chinese food that Brian was fond of. He liked Indian dishes as well and his journalist friend Vince Wilson used to make curries for him and would bring them in plastic containers. Italian food was also popular, especially when Brian could get together with friends at the same time. When one of Forest's matches was called-off due to the weather and the resulting state of the pitch, we all went to the Italian restaurant Trattoria Antonio on Trent Bridge, near the City Ground. There must have been about a dozen of us there, including Brian, and we had a lovely afternoon. That restaurant was usually a meeting place before a game and Brian would ask Michael Keeling and myself to entertain his friends there, including the England cricketer Geoff Boycott and the journalist John Sadler.

As far as more traditional English food is concerned, Brian was once asked to describe his favourite three-course meal. The organiser of a charity cookbook had contacted him and he replied that his menu would start with smoked salmon, followed by saddle of lamb and finished off with home-made rice pudding. Brian also loved various meat pies I used to bring to his house when I worked at Pork Farms. With my boss' permission, I would take a box of lovely pies and give some to Brian. I would be standing in his kitchen and he'd say: "Just put them in the fridge, Col, if you can find any room!" It was my small way of thanking Brian for all the opportunities he had given me over the years. One of his favourites was a chicken pie which was one of the many different types we made at the factory. It was a deep-filled pie and Brian told me that when he cooked it he didn't bother with any gravy – he got a tin of chicken soup instead and poured it over the pie. "You ought to try it sometime," he'd tell me. It would be quite a rich combination, with the soup and the pie together, but he loved it. Years before that, when I worked as a chief engineer at Walkers in Leicester, I would bring him boxes of crisps, again with the firm's permission. You can imagine how popular I was with Brian's children at the time, when they saw all the bags of crisps I'd brought with me.

Fish and chips were also one of Brian's favourites. There was one particular night that I will always remember, when we visited an upmarket fish and chip restaurant in Nottingham. A small group of us were at the City Ground in the evening and the subject of food was mentioned. We were all hungry and the Forest secretary Ken Smales suggested we could all go out and have some fish and chips. Brian was particularly keen on this idea and it was agreed we would drive to a restaurant about ten minutes away in an area known as Canning Circus, on the outskirts of the city centre. Circus was probably the right word – as I ended-up feeling like a right clown by the end of the night!

I drove Brian and a few others to the restaurant, parked the car and walked in. As we waited to order at the takeaway section, I suddenly felt very unwell. Luckily, seeing that I was in the company of Brian, the restaurant owners kindly allowed me to use their toilet, even though we were just having a takeaway. Without going into too much detail, let's just say I was very ill. In fact, I felt so bad that I blacked out. I woke to find myself sitting, leaning against the wall in the toilet. I quickly sorted myself out and opened the door – only to stumble straight into complete darkness. This is very strange, I thought, it's totally quiet. Not a word from the restaurant, not a sound from the kitchen. The place had obviously closed for the night and I was locked inside.

I stepped forward and suddenly felt myself falling several feet to the bottom of some stairs. I lay on my side and looked up. Through a side window I could see the neighbouring police station and then all kinds of worrying thoughts went through my head. What if I was caught and they thought I was a burglar? My whole sorry story of passing out in the toilet would be my only defence. How would I ever live this down? Especially when Brian found out! Luckily I wasn't badly injured from my fall down the steps and after a few minutes of walking around, I managed to find a door, which said 'Fire Escape' on it. I realised that was the only way I was going to get out and avoid spending the night with a load of frozen fish. So I took a deep breath and went for it. I took several quick steps forward, put out both my hands to push the emergency bar downwards – and the door opened. Thank goodness for that – or so I thought, because worse was to come.

I walked to my car, only to discover it had been vandalised – only a few hundred yards from the police station! By this time, it was about two-o-clock in the morning and I flagged down a taxi, which took me home. I was so relieved to walk through my own front door that I just collapsed onto the settee and fell asleep. The next morning, my wife Irene asked why I'd slept on the couch. "Oh, it was quite late and I didn't want to wake you," I said, trying to cover the tracks of my disastrous night. I phoned a colleague who gave me a lift to work and we managed to get my car and sort out the damage. My colleagues were very good about it and even helped repair the car. Fortunately, I didn't have to tell them the whole story of the eventful night. But that wasn't the case where Brian was concerned. The next time I saw him and the others at Forest, they wanted to know what had happened to me. They thought I had just walked off and left them at the restaurant (remember, this was in the days before everybody had mobile phones in their pockets and so they couldn't contact me). I had to confess that I'd passed out in the toilet and must have been in there for hours, until the owners closed for the night. Telling the story a few days afterwards, I could laugh about it. I think there were tears running down Brian's face as I recalled stumbling around in the dark, trying to get out. And for months, if not years, afterwards Brian would always say, "Hey Col, tell us about that time you were locked in at the restaurant!" I was only too happy to oblige and would often embellish the story to suit whoever's company we were in. We would always have a great laugh about it.

In our quiet moments, away from the public glare, Brian also loved talking about food in general. It was probably a good way for him to switch-off from all the pressures of football management. He was quite handy in the kitchen and I think he would have been brilliant appearing on one of the many celebrity chef programmes that fill the television schedules these days. Irene and I were treated to his culinary skills after we had all enjoyed an outdoor concert at Markeaton Park in Derby. Afterwards we were among a few friends that Brian and Barbara invited back to their house. It was a lovely day and we sat in the garden while Brian rustled up some food in the kitchen. He would sometimes have a look in the larder and find something he could turn into a tasty dish. But on this occasion it wasn't just one dish, he kept bringing out tray after tray of lovely food - and he loved doing it.

By complete coincidence, during Brian's early years at Forest I wrote a letter comparing him to the best chef in the world. Having followed his success at Derby, and then seen the disastrous spell at Leeds United after that, I used food as a theme for the letter which looked ahead to exciting times at the City Ground. I described how, at Derby, 'Chef Clough' had started to prepare a wonderful meal to treat all the supporters. They had enjoyed the appetisers and a few delicious main courses before taking a break from the meal to allow all the fine food to digest. Now that Brian had joined Forest, we were tasting all the very best food – lobster, pheasant, you name it, it was on our plate. My letter's food-theme continued. I wrote that, as the dishes for the main courses were being taken away, we were all left wondering what was going to be served up for desert. I had originally written the letter for my friend Michael Keeling, but he passed it on to Brian and he was fascinated by it. He told me he thought it was wonderful. I think it's safe to say that Forest fans were able to savour some extremely enjoyable and flavoursome dishes in the subsequent years – the sweet taste of success.

8.

Brian and Peter

"I've missed him. He used to make me laugh. He was the best diffuser of a situation I have ever known. I hope he's alright." Those quotes from Brian about his old pal Peter Taylor clearly show how much he regretted not making-up with him before Peter died. Their bitter falling-out has been well documented over the years. But I still regret not being able to bring the two of them together to finally make their peace during the separate holidays they both enjoyed in later years in Majorca.

The bitterness of their split meant a reconciliation just wasn't going to happen. Peter had retired from Forest towards the end of the season in 1982. He said he'd had enough. The Reds had gone through a lean spell when they won just one point from five games, culminating in a 1–0 home defeat at the hands of Manchester United. Big money signings like Justin Fashanu, Ian Wallace and Peter Ward hadn't worked-out well and Forest finished twelfth in the First Division. In the previous season, the Reds had been eliminated from the European Cup by CSKA Sofia in the first round.

Looking back, it's easy to say the European Cup winning squad was broken-up too quickly. With Brian as manager and Peter as his trusted assistant, they had both enjoyed tremendous success, beating the odds not once but twice. They then seemed to take a calculated decision to break-up the team so they could re-charge the squad with new blood and push-on again for more glory. But some of the new signings just didn't match what had gone before, with many of Forest's European stars being allowed to leave. The superb Garry Birtles, who had scored his debut goal in the European Cup and ran his legs off during the second European Cup Final against Hamburg, was sold to Manchester United. I remember being in the Forest guest room when Brian called for Garry to join him there and told him United were ready to do a deal. He asked Garry if he wanted to move to Old Trafford and the player confirmed he did. It was seen as a big move for him, but later Brian turned to me and said: "That poor lad." I'm not sure if Brian could envisage the tough time Garry would have at United, but I know he was very glad to re-sign him several seasons later and watch him forge a potent partnership with his son Nigel.

As well as Garry's departure, Tony Woodcock had already joined Cologne in Germany, Martin O'Neill was sold to Norwich, Larry Lloyd went into management at Wigan and later John McGovern became player-manager at Bolton. There were other significant departures including Archie Gemmill, Frank Clark and Ian Bowyer. It is very difficult to maintain the level of success that a provincial club like Forest had achieved – and so it proved to be a mammoth task to live-up to all the expectation. The difficult times were bound to follow and in 1982 Peter felt he'd had enough and wanted to leave Forest. I had a suspicion he wanted to step-down after a conversation we had during a meal at a hotel in Paddington. Peter told me this was the same place where he had suffered a heart attack during a previous visit. He told me he had felt the pain of the attack, although he had not realised what it was at the time. I think he must have been considering the prospect of stepping-down when he told me this, because not long afterwards he told Brian that he wanted to retire. It was obviously on his mind and he wanted to talk to me about it. Peter's departure seemed quite amicable and Brian said he would make sure that Forest looked after his mate in the deal that was agreed for him to leave.

A few months later, Peter decided to become manager of Derby County. He must have felt there was unfinished business there and I

Cover image, presenting Brian with a bottle of champagne

Centre stage in the school football team. I am centre of the front row in the Mortimer Wilson School team in Alfreton.

Above: My FA Cup Final ticket for 1969

Left: Ready for work at Morton Colliery

DERBY COUNTY FOOTBALL CLUB LTD.

BRIAN CLOUGH, (*Manager*)
C. ANNABLE, (*Secretary*)

Telegraphic Address:—"FOOTBALL DERBY"
Telephone:—DERBY 44850.

BASEBALL GROUND DERBY

DE3 8NB

20th December, 1967.

Mr. T. Shields,

Dear Mr. Shields,

    Thank you for your letter, please find enclosed herewith one seat ticket for our match against Leeds United on Wednesday, 17th January.

    I think that anybody who has been a supporter of Derby County for forty five years deserves a break so we will stand the cost of the seat.

    I hope you enjoy the match and thank you for your good wishes.

Yours sincerely

Brian Clough

Brian's letter to my Dad

Left: Ram man. Holding the Derby County mascot at a supporters club meeting. Right: My Dad with his trophies for showing caged birds

Enjoying Derby's trip to Lisbon with my roommate Johnnie Birch.

Derby County tickets for European Cup ties

My daughter Susan with her husband Neil in June 1979.

Above: Enjoying the Cala Millor sunshine. That's me (second left) with Brian, Percy Simmons and Michael Keeling

Left: Brian on the deck of a naval boat during our trip to Malta

Above: Arms folded, Brian was uncomfortable on board the boat. Forest's Ian Wallace is in the foreground of this picture

Left: Me at the wheel of the Maltese naval boat

At a Maltese restaurant with friends from Forest. I am far right; Brian is second left, waving

Trophy Man. Me with Forest trophies, the League Championship, Charity Shield and League Cup

With my friend and former Forest photographer Charlie Noble, whose camera captured some great occasions over the years

Mum with Brian

Mum with former Derby player Willie Carlin, who has remained a good friend

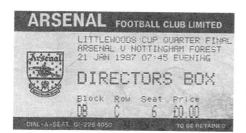

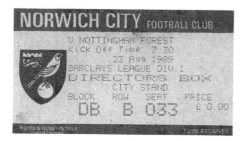

Bottom left previous page and this page: A selection of Directors' Box tickets and passes – I felt like a football millionaire!

*My programme
from Forest's first
European Cup Final
victory.*

*The programme from
Forest's victory over
Vorwarts*

President:
H.W. Alcock, F.C.A.

Directors:
G.E. Macpherson, J.P. (Chairman)
F. Reacher (Vice-Chairman)
G.T. Thorpe
F.T.C. Pell, F.C.A.
D.C.Pavis
M. Roworth
J.F. Hickling
F.A. Allcock
I.I. Korn

Secretary:
Ken Smales

FOUNDED 1865

NOTTINGHAM FOREST
Football Club Ltd.

Reg. Office:
City Ground
Nottingham NG2 5JF

Reg. in England No. 1630402

Telephone 822202
Information Desk 821122
Pools Office 820444

Telegrams
Forestball Nottingham

Manager:
Brian H. Clough

Monday, 26th September, 1983.

The Directors, Management, and Players are pleased to welcome
you aboard their chartered flight to the German Democratic
Republic.

Have a good trip, enjoy the game, and join us again soon.

G. E. Macpherson, J.P.

CHAIRMAN

Forest letter. A welcoming letter for my trip to Vorwarts in the UEFA Cup in 1983. We won 1–0.

Celebrating a family birthday with Brian and my brother
Trevor in Forest's Jubilee Club

A precious gift. The tie Brian gave me bearing his initials

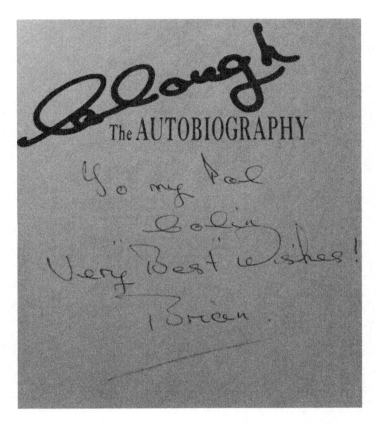

Brian's personal message to me in his first autobiography

think he assumed Brian would join him, even though Peter had said he was retiring. I think there had been previous attempts to lure the pair back to Derby, but I was not involved in any discussions about that. However, I do know that Brian would not have returned to Derby while certain people were still there, following his controversial resignation. Soon after Peter went to Derby, the two sides played each other in the FA Cup and Derby beat Forest. That wasn't a happy day to say the least. But what made things one hundred times worse was when Peter signed John Robertson without telling Brian. Now, if there's one thing that Brian always emphasised, it was loyalty. Robertson himself was not at fault, but Brian felt that Peter had been disloyal by not picking-up the phone and telling him about signing the player who had been so instrumental in Forest winning two European Cups. Brian used to say: "If you're loyal, you're loyal – if you're not, you're not." To him, it was as simple as that. He felt Peter had betrayed him and, being someone who always spoke his mind, he didn't hide his feelings about the matter. They never spoke to each other again.

As the years went by, Brian admitted that he missed Peter. He once said to me: "I just wish he'd pop his head in to my office and say hello. I wish he'd come and see Nigel play – he taught Nigel so much about the game." I thought to myself that, maybe, Peter did see Nigel play – and not necessarily at the City Ground. Peter was the master of disguise and could go along to games to watch players and no one would recognise him. I'd like to think that perhaps he went to see Nigel play in the Forest first team at some point, under the cover of some disguise. I always got on very well with Peter and I helped to find work at the Co-op Bakery for his brothers. After his spell at Derby, which didn't work out very well, I would often see him on holiday in Cala Millor in Majorca. Peter or his wife, Lilian, would occasionally phone me to arrange a supply of black pudding, or other food like that, for them to take with them.

Both Brian and Peter continued to love that sunshine resort but, because of their falling-out, they now went there separately. The pair of them were only a couple of streets away from each other when I saw Peter and he asked me: "How's he doing? Is he alright?" He was referring to Brian of course and I replied that he was fine. Knowing that Brian was relaxing just a short distance away, I added: "Why don't you come round? I'm just about to meet him." Peter declined the offer – he said he and his wife were going shopping. I followed it up with another attempt: "He'd love to see you, Peter, why don't you come round – we're going to that cafe around the corner." But Peter declined the offer again. "Not just now," he said. I said farewell to Peter and then went to see Brian. When the moment was right – when it was just Brian and me alone – I told him what had happened.

"I've just seen your mate," I said.

"Who's that?" Brian replied, even though I think he knew who I was referring to.

"Peter of course," I said.

"Is he alright?" asked Brian.

I said he was. But unfortunately my efforts to bring them together didn't come to anything. If Brian had been sitting on his own, may be Peter would have walked round to see him. But he knew Brian would be with lots of other people (there was always a group of us there, sometimes seven or eight, at other times it could be as many as 14). While I know Peter and Lilian would have been genuinely welcomed if they had gone to see Brian, it just wasn't in Peter's nature to walk into that situation with a group of people.

In many ways Brian and Peter were like chalk and cheese – but perhaps that's why they got on so well. Brian loved the limelight but Peter would shy away from it. On one occasion I picked Peter up from his house and took him to a dinner at the Pennine Hotel in Derby. We were chatting away on the journey there and when we got near the hotel he said: "When we get out of this car I don't want you to move an inch away from me until we have sat down at the table." It was an indication of how uncomfortable he could be with groups of people he didn't know. So that evening I stuck to him like a blanket and made sure I kept him company.

On another visit to Majorca, I saw Peter again and stopped to have a chat. It was at a time when Forest (without him) were planning a tour of Australia. Peter said to me: "Tell Brian, it's wrong – they shouldn't be doing it. They won't have enough time to recover from it." I couldn't believe Peter actually wanted me to pass this message on to Brian. Who knows, I could have become a go-between if they had decided to use me in that way. It would have been so good if I had managed to get them back together by being the messenger. There was certainly mutual trust between me and both of them. I wouldn't have gone blabbing about it to the media – and they knew that. I would have felt so proud if I could have re-united them. But eventually any hopes of a reconciliation ended when Peter died. In October 1990, I went with Brian and Barbara to Peter's funeral. I think Brian was overwhelmed by it all because, in his heart, he would have liked to have made it up with Peter, despite all the bitterness and what had been said. It's strange how strong friendships can turn that way. When those kind of relationships go wrong, the bitterness can be so much stronger. I think that's what killed any hope of them getting back together.

Brian continued to emphasise the importance of loyalty and he remained loyal to Forest and the supporters, even though there were times he may have been tempted away. He was determined to bring more success to the club, although he was still hot property and everyone wanted a piece of him. There was always someone trying to poach him. At one stage, there was even talk of him leaving to manage Wales. A group of Welsh celebrities backed the idea and Brian suggested doing it on a part-time basis, keeping his role at the City Ground. But it didn't come to anything. I think Brian was reluctant to let go of what he was creating at Forest, despite not having all the resources that managers like Alex Ferguson have had at their disposal in recent years. The club needed a lot of inward investment, which just wasn't there. In those days, Forest had a committee structure, rather than a board of directors, and I can imagine there was a lot of nervousness among the members of the committee about keeping the club solvent because they were essentially the under-writers. When the Executive Stand (now Brian Clough Stand) was built, the sale of the striker Peter Davenport to Manchester United helped to pay for it. As far as I know, the likes of Alex Ferguson and the other so-called top managers have not been in a position where they have had to do that to keep a club afloat.

The former Aston Villa chairman Doug Ellis was an admirer of Brian and I got the impression he would have liked him to become manager at Villa Park. Whenever we went there for a Forest match, Michael Keeling and I were treated like VIP's because we were Brian's friends. We would always have the best seats in the Directors' Box. Brian would say to me: "We're at Villa tonight, you'll be able to have whatever you like." If Brian had become Villa manager, I think Doug Ellis would have enjoyed it initially, but the chemistry between the two of them would have been explosive – and I mean destructive – because they were both strong characters. I just don't think it would have been a good combination at all. But we enjoyed some good trips to Villa and it was there that I met the violinist Nigel Kennedy, who is a big Villa fan, and got to know him. When his team came to play at the City Ground he wanted to join me and some friends in the guest room, but he wasn't allowed in because there was a strict dress code and he wasn't wearing a tie. So we arranged to get a spare tie for him and he was so appreciative that he invited us to his concert in Nottingham. "Thank you guys," he said. "I'm not used to getting dressed up for football. They don't ask me to wear a tie at Villa." He had brought a little dog with him, which he was carrying under his arm, and we enjoyed chatting before kick-off, at half-time and after the game.

One job offer that Brian would have accepted without hesitation was the chance to be England manager. He was the people's choice and it was a scandal that the Football Association didn't choose him. But, as he admitted himself, the FA wouldn't have been able to deal with him. He would have run the show from top to bottom. And we would have won a few trophies along the way. In his heart he knew they would never appoint him. But on one occasion he thought he had got the job. Michael Keeling took him down to the FA headquarters at Lancaster Gate for the interview. He came out of it thinking he had done well, but they gave the job to Ron Greenwood. Yet Brian was head and shoulders above Ron Greenwood as far as football management was concerned. You just had to look at what Brian had won as a club manager. His record blew his rivals out of the water. But the decision-makers were out of touch with what the fans wanted. To put it simply, they couldn't have handled Brian, it didn't matter what abilities he had as a manager.

There were also calls for Brian to be England boss when Sir Bobby Robson got the role. Sir Bobby was a lovely man and I remember meeting him when he was manager of Ipswich. Brian, Michael and I went into his office at Portman Road and he made us feel at home. But when he and Brian started talking about football I didn't understand a word of it – it was all technical jargon as far as I was concerned! I saw Sir Bobby again a few years later when he had been appointed England manager. We were at Villa Park and he was there assessing players. I was there with Michael and of course, in our opinion, Brian should have been given the top job. We felt he was far better equipped to do it. As a result, there was some friendly banter on that subject between Michael and Sir Bobby, but he could handle it and entered into the spirit of things, giving us some chitchat back.

While Brian would no doubt have attracted controversy as England boss, he would have breathed new life into football. There would have been big changes within the organisation of the game and I think the officials were afraid of that. He would have ended the tradition of 'the men in suits' having all the power. Brian would have been very protective of his players and no official in an England blazer would have been allowed in his dressing room when he was with the team. That was very much his domain and there would have been no place for FA officials or directors of this and that. That dressing room door would have been closed to every one of them – unless they were invited.

There are other aspects of the job he would have had strong opinions about too. I don't think he would have liked to hear the fans playing musical instruments throughout England matches. Well, maybe at half-time, but certainly not during the game. It's noticeable that the noisy music-makers with their trumpets and drums are nowhere near the FA hierarchy. Instead, they are playing next to fans, who have paid good money to enjoy the game without a trumpet blowing in their ears. Brian didn't like any interference while he was trying to do his job – just as he didn't like intruders on the pitch. Take, for example, those incidents when he dragged a man dressed as a clown off the pitch or clipped those fans round the ear when they ran-on after the final whistle. I could completely understand why he did that, even though he served a touchline ban after one of the incidents. Brian took the game very seriously and it made him angry when he saw it trivialised by some people. It was his living and it meant everything to him. Is football as important as life and death? Well, my next story will shed some light on that.

9.

Tragedy At Christmas

It is still very difficult to come to terms with the death of my daughter, Susan, even though it is now many years since she passed away. The sudden nature of her death made it all the more painful and did not give us the chance to say goodbye. Susan was just thirty-one years old when she died. She was pregnant with what would have been her first child and had a wonderful life still ahead of her. We had all been looking forward to celebrating Christmas together, but instead we held her funeral on Christmas Eve.

At the time, football seemed a world away from the devastation both Irene and I felt at losing our daughter unexpectedly. No parent expects to have to bury a child. But a quote comes to mind from the former Liverpool manager, Bill Shankly, who I was lucky enough to know. He was once reported as saying something along the lines of: "Some people believe football is a matter of life and death, I am very disappointed with that attitude. I can assure you it is much more important than that." Whether that assessment is true or not, I will let you decide. But what I *can* say is that football, and my friends at Nottingham Forest including Brian Clough, certainly helped me cope with what was a terrible and agonising tragedy.

Susan was about eight months pregnant and phoned us one evening, just a few days before Christmas. I remember it as a busy time at work for both Irene and myself, coming up to the festive period. Susan called us to say she was at the hospital, but not to worry. She had been to see her GP because she had noticed that one of her ankles was a bit swollen. Susan had faced some difficulty getting pregnant, so the doctors felt it was important to keep an eye on her. She was already having treatment through the local GP and they clearly did not want to take any chances about a swollen ankle. So they referred her to the hospital and that is when Susan phoned us to say that she was alright. She said there was nothing to worry about, but they might keep her in hospital overnight. That night I thought about her as I went to bed and said a little prayer, hoping everything would be OK for her. But the following morning, at about six-o-clock, there was a phone call from the hospital. Irene took the call and told me that we had to get to the hospital because Susan wasn't well. It was like a bolt from the blue.

"What's all this about, then?" I asked Irene.

"I don't know, but we've got to get there as soon as possible," she replied.

We quickly got dressed and I drove us to the hospital, where we headed for the maternity department. We were greeted by a woman who said: "Mr and Mrs Shields, we've tried everything we can, but your daughter is not very well at all. Can you wait in this room for me please?"

The next thing I knew is that we were being told that Susan had passed away. I just couldn't believe it. I couldn't comprehend the words I had just heard. Susan's husband, Neil, and my youngest son David were both there too. It was a very emotional time. We were told that we could go and see her, but I decided not to. I just couldn't face that situation. The others went to see her, but while they were gone a nurse approached me with a plastic bag containing Susan's belongings.

I was in a state of shock, completely lost for words, as the painful reality began to hit me. I slowly walked back to my car, sat in the driver's seat and opened the plastic bag. Inside was Susan's flannel, which was still wet. At that point, I lost control of my emotions and collapsed in a heap. I simply could not understand how a young woman in Susan's position could be admitted to hospital one evening and then be dead the following morning. How could she be at work, as a barrister's clerk, one day and then not with us, the next? And I still can't comprehend it to this day. The medical experts told us that she had a tumour on her adrenalin gland. As a result, the tumour had 'excited' the gland and she had suffered a heart attack. Since then, I have asked lots of questions about it and sought the very best advice I can get, but I feel no further forward. There will always be a massive gap in our lives without Susan. The medics were also unable to save her baby, which made the circumstances even more painful.

Susan was cremated on Christmas Eve, 1987 – coincidentally, our wedding anniversary. As you can imagine, it was the worst Christmas that Irene and I have ever experienced. Somehow, with the help of our family, we got through it and I received a phone call from Michael Keeling. It was completely unexpected, but he said that he and Brian would like me to travel down to the Forest match at Arsenal on Boxing Day, if I wanted to. Both Michael and Brian knew about Susan's death and they were asking me to go as their friend. They knew it would be a distraction from the turmoil I was facing. Michael had suffered a similar agony a few years before with the loss of his daughter, Julie, when she was a young woman. She had been a very bubbly young lady and was loved by everyone who met her. I think sharing that same kind of loss strengthened the bond between us. I told Michael that I would like to join him at the Boxing Day match. Irene insisted that I should go to the game, as it was something that Susan would have wanted me to do. She was a keen football fan and had met Brian several times. They had got on really well and, from time to time, she and her husband Neil went into his office to say hello.

On Boxing Day morning I walked to the City Ground from my home about half a mile away. As Brian had already travelled down to Highbury on the team bus, Michael was waiting for me in the car park. Arrangements had been made for us to travel on the directors' coach, which was about to leave. It wasn't the first time I had joined the directors on their bus. Sometimes, if Brian and Michael were meeting up in London for business reasons and needed to leave a couple of days before a game, I would be invited on the directors' coach and travel with them. On this particular day, I was worried that I wouldn't be much company on the trip, after all that had happened. But the directors, including the chairman Maurice Roworth, were absolutely fantastic. A bottle of champagne suddenly appeared and it was given to me with a few glasses. Michael opened it and thankfully it helped to lighten the mood as we started to make our way down to London. Later on in the journey, another bottle appeared. They really looked after me well that day and tried to lift my spirits. In fact, everyone at the club, including the players, were wonderful around that time and helped me get through a horrible period in my life. Even now, it is hard to think that I'll never see Susan again. Instead, I like to think that she is still just down the road, pottering about and getting on with her life. That's the only way I can deal with it. I take Irene to the churchyard where Susan's ashes are buried, but I can't walk with her to the plot. I stay in the car at the bottom of the driveway and have my own little chat with Susan. Just a father and his daughter sharing their own special time together.

*   *   *

In the same way that I received help to cope with the death of Susan, I did my best to support Brian when his close friend Stuart Dryden died. Stuart had been chairman of Nottingham Forest and was instrumental in bringing Brian to the club, even though he was not chairman at that particular time. What an achievement that was, paving the way to one of the most remarkable stories that football has ever seen. Brian would often talk to Stuart about football. A lot of their conversations were about the game and Brian valued Stuart's opinion, which was generally unusual for a club director where Brian was concerned. I remember hearing one conversation where Stuart was giving Brian his views about a Forest defender. "He jumps too soon," was Stuart's verdict about this particular player's heading ability. As far as I was concerned, it was not something I had noticed, but it showed how Stuart analysed the game and the abilities of individual players.

Brian thought the world of Stuart and remained loyal to him during and after a court case in which Stuart was jailed for a financial offence at the Post Office he ran in the village of Ruddington. Knowing what a good friend he was of Brian's, I mentioned that a friend of mine, Roy Fletcher from Leicester, worked as a prison officer. I offered to see if I could arrange something to make Stuart's time in prison a little more comfortable. As a result, Roy was able to sort-out a small amount of preferential treatment and secured permission for Stuart to have a radio. Brian hadn't asked for any special treatment for his friend, but he appreciated Roy's help and gave him the nickname 'Leicester' simply because that is where he was from.

Whenever he saw Roy, Brian would shout: "Hey, Leicester, are you alright?" Roy loved it. He described to me how Brian had spotted him in the City Ground car park and called over to him: "Hey, Leicester, what are you up to?" Roy explained he was waiting for me and Michael Keeling. "Not out here, you're not," replied Brian. "Come and wait inside, they'll come and find you." They also bumped into each other at East Midlands Airport, as Roy and his wife Marion were heading out to Cyprus and Brian was returning from a trip to Majorca. Once again came the friendly greeting: "Hey, Leicester, are you alright? Make sure you have a good holiday!" Roy was originally a Derby fan, but he became a Forest convert and bought a season ticket. One of his colleagues became so enthusiastic about going to the City Ground with him that when he died his ashes were scattered there.

After Stuart was released from jail, he would often join us in the guest room at the City Ground on match days. Brian would talk to him about football and ask him what he thought about particular players. There was still a good rapport between them. They both loved cricket and on a few occasions I went with them to watch matches at Trent Bridge. There would be an open invitation for me to join them. In later years, Brian said he hoped that the loyalty he showed Stuart at a time of great distress (the court case) was as comforting as the faith and friendship that Stuart had always extended to him. It's therefore not surprising that when Stuart died, it hit Brian really hard. Shortly after we received the sad news, Michael and I picked Brian up from his home to take him to a hotel just outside Coventry, where the Forest team was staying. Brian was clearly devastated about Stuart's death and I did my best to console him as we travelled in the car. By the time we reached the hotel, he was feeling a little brighter but I think he was doing what he could to hide his grief.

I'd like to think I was able to help Brian during the difficult time of losing a close friend and, in doing so, earned his respect. Brian never forgot who his friends were. Another friendship he valued was that of the head gardener at Darley Abbey Park, David Gregory, who would often join the trips to Cala Millor. At one of the many sporting dinners we attended around Britain, Brian arranged for David to sit next to the former Welsh international John Charles. As far as David was concerned, he was sitting next to a legend. Charles was known as the Gentle Giant because of his stature (he was over six-feet tall) and honourable play (I believe he was never cautioned or sent off during his career). He was one of the first British players to transfer to a foreign league when he joined Juventus in 1957. David thought it was marvellous to be able to chat with him. I think it was Brian's way of putting 'the ordinary man' in circumstances he could only have dreamt about. It was just like the time he had asked me to look after Bill Shankly as we prepared to have lunch before a Forest game. On another occasion, Brian led me towards the long room at Wembley Stadium, where all the Football Association directors were gathering before an England match. He said to Michael and I: "Get yourself in there, you're more entitled to be there than any of them. Go and help yourself." There was a huge buffet spread out over a number of tables. Brian told the officials on the door:

"I'd like you to let these people in – they're my friends." To Brian, it was all about sharing – and there are so many more examples of his generosity.

10.

A Trip To See Sinatra – His Way

Wherever Brian went, he seemed to have a special aura around him. When he walked into a room full of people, the atmosphere would dramatically change, like a sudden charge of electricity, and the place would be buzzing. Even after he retired, there would be tremendous excitement when Brian paid a visit. I would spot people suddenly picking-up their mobile phones to tell their friends that they were in the same place as Brian Clough. Sometimes Brian would approach them and ask: "Are you phoning home to tell them that I'm here? Well, give me that phone for a minute." He'd then hold their mobile phone so he could speak to the bemused person on the other end of the conversation. They would suddenly hear that famous voice, as he asked: "Is he telling you that Brian's here?" Before the other person could answer, he would add: "Well, he's absolutely right, this is Brian. How are you?" He would then have a quick conversation with the stranger before handing the phone back. The person on the other end of the line must have been so shocked – and delighted. The owner of the phone would be on cloud nine, with a tale to tell all their family and friends. They would be able to dine out on that story for years to come.

Brian was usually very generous in giving his time to fans, but he didn't like it when people tried to sneak-up on him. Sometimes we would be sitting and having a chat, perhaps playing dominoes or cards, and he would spot someone trying to take a sneaky photograph. He didn't like that at all. He would tell them that if they wanted a photo they should come over to see him and say hello. They would then approach him and Brian would be more than happy to have a photo with them and he would ask how they were. If it was someone with a little child he would always make a fuss of them and pose for a photo. The proud Mum or Dad would sometimes get a kiss on the cheek too!

His appreciation of all football supporters was evident after a match at Portsmouth, which Forest had lost. It was March 1992 and the Reds had just been knocked out of the FA Cup at the quarter-final stage. Brian was sitting on the team coach ready to leave. He wasn't always the last person to get on board and on this occasion he was in his seat before some of the players. A group of fans had gathered near the bus and they were asking the Forest players to sign autographs before the team climbed aboard for the long journey home. Sitting at the front and noticing what was happening, Brian asked Albert the driver whether the door at the back of the coach could be opened. When Albert confirmed it could be, Brian asked him to open it up. He then told all the Portsmouth fans who had been waiting for autographs that they could climb on board to get all the signatures they wanted. Once the players were in their seats, Brian told them: "Now you lot, sign some autographs for these people who've been waiting." Dozens of supporters proceeded to file through the coach, from one end to the other, collecting the autographs of Brian and the players, before getting off the bus through the back door. The whole process lasted about twenty minutes. And this was after Forest had lost! I can't imagine many – if any – club managers doing that sort of thing in those circumstances nowadays. But it demonstrated the strong bond that Brian had with fans from all clubs. They respected him and that respect was amplified one hundred fold after an experience like that. Even though the team coach was hallowed ground as far as Brian was concerned (and I had learned that from my own experience), it wasn't the only time he allowed fans onto the coach to get autographs. The supporters who benefitted from his generosity of spirit were absolutely amazed and delighted.

Brian always had a lot of time for children, the elderly and disabled people. I've lost count of the occasions we would go to special schools to present wheelchairs for which he had raised the money. Whenever he could support a charity that he considered worthwhile, he would do so. One of the many good causes we attended was for the SportsAid Foundation, which was set-up to help the sporting stars of tomorrow. They had organised a fund-raising dinner at County Hall in Nottingham, with the Olympic star Sebastian Coe and entertainer Dickie Henderson among the guests. Brian was determined to be present too, even though I think it had been quite a rush for him to get there. He turned to my wife and said: "Look here, Irene," and he hitched-up the bottom of his trouser leg to reveal that a small hole had suddenly appeared in his shoe. "Look at my shoe," said Brian with a smile. "This is the state I'm in. What will everyone think of me?" Irene smiled back and said: "Well, they won't see it, will they?" And that was quite true of course. The people at the dinner were just delighted that Brian had been able to get there and help them raise more money for a good cause. I am convinced that the very fact Brian attended that event meant that the organisers could sell considerably more tickets than they had expected, raising even more cash for young people.

When we were on holiday abroad, Brian would sometimes spot a young child with their Mum or Dad, eyeing-up the toys at the shops on the seafront. Brian would walk up to the family and offer to buy them a bucket and spade, or whatever toy the youngster liked. He would get some bewildered looks from parents who were from other countries and perhaps didn't quite know who he was (especially seeing him out of context). But the British families loved it. It was simply Brian being generous – he wanted youngsters to enjoy the seaside in the same way he had enjoyed family holidays in Blackpool when he was a little lad.

The value of sharing things was always important to Brian – and I don't mean just money. He wanted people to experience many of the exciting opportunities that he enjoyed. For example, there was the night I saw Frank Sinatra. It's well-known that Brian loved Sinatra's songs. I would often hear him sing them, whether it was at the City Ground or in the car. As a Sinatra fan myself, I was invited by Brian to a special concert at the Royal Albert Hall in London. It starred Sinatra, Sammy Davis Junior and Liza Minnelli. Brian had already been to see the show, but he still organised a trip for a group of us to travel down to the capital and see these three singing stars perform. On the night, Michael Keeling and I were sitting a few rows from the front, where Brian would have sat if he had been there. Irene and Michael's wife, Ann, were sitting in one of the posh boxes. Throughout that evening, I couldn't help thinking that although we were watching three legends perform on stage, Michael and I were also in superb company among the audience, as we were surrounded by celebrities. There were stars from the world of show business and sport. I felt lucky to be sitting next to Sir Bobby Robson who was clearly a Sinatra fan. At one point in the show, Old Blue Eyes actually mentioned Brian and pointed to where Michael and I were sitting, thinking that Brian was sitting there. It all seemed quite surreal, but it was a fantastic event. If only Brian had been there himself – it would have made his night to have heard Sinatra refer to him personally. The whole trip must have cost Brian a fortune, but I was determined to pay my own way. So several days later I went down to the City Ground to see him. As he was walking back from the training ground, I told him I had come to pay for my tickets. "Hey, thanks very much Col," he said. "You're the only one who's paid me." I know he didn't expect the money from me, and hadn't asked for it, but I didn't want it to appear that I was taking advantage of the situation. The sheer experience of being at the show, and among such wonderful company, had been priceless as far as I was concerned.

Some of Brian's favourite songs like *Fly Me To The Moon* and *You Make Me Feel So Young* were also top of the list when we enjoyed another night out – only this time they were performed by a Sinatra impersonator.

Irene and I had received an invitation to join Brian and Barbara for a get-together at the Risley Hall Hotel, near junction 25 of the M1 in Derbyshire. We thought it was going to be a small gathering of friends, but when we arrived the place was absolutely buzzing. We sat at the same table as Archie and Betty Gemmill, who have remained friends. The focal point of the night was a Frank Sinatra tribute act. Brian was really impressed by this particular singer because not only did he sound like Sinatra, he had all the little mannerisms too. He was so good that some people in the audience thought he must have been miming, but Brian and I refused to believe that. We both thought he was brilliant. It was so enjoyable that Brian was humming away with some of the tunes. When it came to the lyrics of Sinatra songs, he knew many of them word-for-word. On other occasions, when there was a group of us, we would often have little singsongs together. He didn't like 'My Way' too much, even though many people associate him with the lyrics of that song. Another of his favourites was 'Let's Face the Music and Dance' – and he would love to emphasise the opening words of it: "There may be trouble ahead ..." I think that line struck a chord with him because it seemed to sum-up perfectly the unpredictable nature of football.

Even when Brian was away from the public spotlight, and doing ordinary things, he still had that special aura around him. He loved doing the types of things that everyone else liked to do. When he found out that I was a member of the Royal British Legion and that I often visited his local branch of the organisation, he was keen to come along too. As a former serviceman, the legion has always been very close to my heart. Over the last fifty years, I've held various official positions within the legion and have been very proud to do so. Brian's friend David Gregory invited me along to the RBL's club at Darley Abbey, a village on the outskirts of Derby and not far from where Brian lived at the time. Although I was living in Nottingham, I thought nothing of regularly driving down the A52 (now the Brian Clough Way) to Derby to meet David there and spend the evenings playing snooker and dominoes. "Why don't you ask me to come along?" enquired Brian when he discovered where we going. From that moment, we all made it a regular visit, with Michael coming along too.

Unfortunately, not all was going well behind the scenes at this particular branch of the legion. A friend told me it was facing financial difficulties and the officials were on the verge of closing it down. Then my friend added: "Did you say that Brian goes there?" I confirmed he did – and not only that, he thoroughly enjoyed his visits there. As a result, my friend made a suggestion: "What if I were to say that if Brian became President of the club, we could have a re-think about it?" So the next time I saw Brian, I asked him if he would consider the position. There was no hesitation. "Of course I will. Anything to help," he told me. Knowing that the branch was on the brink of closing for good, the officials there held an extraordinary meeting and made Brian the President. The club was saved and Brian felt proud about it. He was pleased that all the regulars who went there to socialise over a pint and a game of dominoes were still able to go. Brian was an ex-serviceman himself (he had been in the RAF) and he loved his association with the legion. I thought it was incredible that the presence of one man could have made such a difference – but that is a marvellous example of the influence Brian could have in certain situations. Having such a high-profile figure at the top meant that the club survived.

Brian's role as President of the Darley Abbey branch of the Royal British Legion was purely an honorary position. He loved his evenings at the club, sitting among the members and chatting to them. I could see he felt comfortable there and enjoyed the pass-times of the ordinary working man. Sometimes I would be his snooker partner – but heck, talk about being under pressure! Forget about crucial matches in the European Cup and vital league games where every point counted, even in a game of snooker at a small social club like that, Brian hated to lose. If you made a mistake and missed a shot, he would be breathing down your neck. "What made you play a shot like that?" he would demand to know. There was no time for any messing about and it really kept you on your toes. In moments like that I could see why he got the very best out of his own players.

He was a superb dominoes player too. Sometimes I would play against him and he was still as competitive as ever. He disliked losing at any game. The regulars at the legion would queue-up to play against him. Somehow he had a knack of knowing which dominoes you should and shouldn't play next. "Put that 6–3 down, then," he would tell you. And invariably you would realise that there was no alternative but to play it – and he was right. How he knew what dominoes I was holding still baffles me to this day. If I partnered him at dominoes and played well he would say: "Well done, Col." And then he would lean over towards me and whisper, so only I could hear: "You're not a bad player." That simple comment would make me feel really good. Once again, I could fully appreciate the effect he would have on his football team with a few words of encouragement. When I lived in the Nottinghamshire village of Keyworth, I had a friend called Eric who was in his eighties. He liked playing dominoes and Brian would say: "Bring Eric with you, I like him." Although Eric didn't go to football matches, he loved being in Brian's company.

When the legion developed new premises in Keyworth, after moving out of an old building, I was part of the committee that planned the opening ceremony. We wanted a high-profile event to celebrate the success of the project. The other committee members asked if I could see whether Brian would come along and officially open the building. When I asked him, there was no hesitation. He agreed straightaway. "Just tell me when it is and I'll be there," he said. "Well, if you can just pop your head in and say hello, that would be great," I suggested, knowing how busy and in-demand he was. On the day, Brian surprised us all. Not only was he there to perform the opening ceremony, but he also brought with him a group of Forest players, as well as his assistant Ron Fenton and coach Liam O'Kane. Brian walked into the club and took over the place, in the way only he could. Within a few minutes he was playing darts with the lads while some of the Forest team were playing pool with another group. Brian had a friendly jibe at the senior officials of the legion's club and it went down really well – it was his way of putting everyone on the same level and raising a laugh at the same time. He made a short speech to open the building and then continued socialising with all the members. His involvement that night was much more than I could ever have hoped for, I couldn't believe it. He was, in effect, doing it all for me. What a tremendous night it was – and one which members of the legion often talk about to this day.

But that wasn't the only time that Brian made a special appearance in Keyworth. I was instrumental in arranging a game involving Forest and the local team, Keyworth United. They were run by a former professional player called Arthur Oldham. I knew Arthur and occasionally had a drink with him. One day we were chatting and he said to me: "Wouldn't it be wonderful if we could get Forest to come here and help us to not only raise some money but also raise our profile and put us on the map?" I told Arthur I would see what I could do, but made no promises. Initially, I spoke to Alan Hill, who was part of Brian's backroom staff and lived nearby. He thought a match between the village team and Forest was a great idea and suggested that I have a word with Brian. I was unsure how Brian would react. Making a personal appearance was one thing, but providing players for a full match was quite another. I decided to put my head in the lion's den (that's what it felt like at the time!) and approached Brian about it. I asked whether he would go along to Keyworth United sometime and take a few players for a game, to give the village club a bit of a boost. I was shocked – and utterly delighted – when he agreed. "We'll take the team up there," he said without a second thought. What an amazing day it turned out to be. Brian brought the full Forest first team. To coin a phrase, Arthur Oldham was over the moon about it. Forest had spotted a local player called David

Riley and decided he was worth looking at. He went on to play for the Reds, appearing for the first team occasionally. The match turned-out to be Forest's way of helping out a small club, which had in turn, helped them. When Brian spoke to me about David Riley, he always referred to him as 'your mate,' even though I didn't know him. Ironically, Brian told me he liked 'Biddy' Riley – as he was known by many people – for his general personality more than his playing ability. "He's such an inspiration in the dressing room that I want him to be part of the team," said Brian. "He's willing to do all the jobs, all the fetching and carrying, and the lads love him." On that hot Sunday afternoon in Keyworth, in July 1984, two thousand people gathered to watch him play as part of a Forest team, which included names like Paul Hart, Kenny Swain and Steve Hodge. 'Biddy' scored one of the goals in a two-nil victory.

*   *   *

Over the years, Brian was always very welcoming and generous towards my friends. I'll always be appreciative of that, because some people, who did not know him well, could be apprehensive about meeting him due to his outspoken nature in public. But I can't stress enough how kind and considerate he could be. When I invited some friends over from France, he was keen to meet them and make a fuss of them, even though he could not speak a word of French. My friendship with the foreign visitors had originated from a twinning agreement between the village of Keyworth and a town in northern France. I was part of the inaugural trip to Feignes, organised by the two town councils and involving the Royal British Legion and local veterans. It was 1977 and we took veterans from the First and Second World Wars.

Irene and I were paired with a French couple called Alice and Robert. Although none of us could speak the other's language, a wonderful friendship developed. Robert had fought in the resistance and Alice had been wounded in a bombing raid. As the years went by, their son Alan and daughter-in-law Kathrine began to visit us with their young son, Benoit. Alan loves football and is a Lille supporter. Whenever I mentioned to Brian that I had French visitors staying with us, he would insist that I brought them to watch a match. In fact, they went to several games and on each occasion Brian would invite them into his office and spend time with them. They could not speak much English and they would often sit there looking a little bemused by it all. But Brian's sheer presence and personality would break down the language barrier and he would make sure they had a wonderful time in his company. When it was time to leave, they certainly did not need me to explain how special it had been for them to be with Brian in his office. Not surprisingly, Benoit became a Nottingham Forest supporter at the age of eight and has remained so to this day. He's now twenty-nine.

Brian never forgot people who remained loyal to him and helped him over the years. Even the barber who used to cut the players' hair during the Derby County days would come along to Forest games on a regular basis, at Brian's invitation. It's well known that Brian thought it was important that his players should look smart young men, so he wasn't going to forget Frank the barber!

Brian was also welcoming to my boss, Brian Stein, who joined us at the legion too. At that time he was a young director with Northern Foods and stayed in a hotel when he arrived in Nottingham. But he told me that the hotel was not very comfortable for him, so I decided to find an alternative place for him to stay. Knowing that Brian (Clough) used a hotel called The Windsor Lodge for friends, celebrities and family to stay in, near the City Ground, I asked the couple who ran it whether they could arrange alternative accommodation. They were able to find him a room there and he loved it. I told Brian (Clough) about it and he suggested that I bring the new boss to the legion for the night. Brian Stein was absolutely delighted and became a regular visitor and dominoes player. He is a Liverpool fan and Brian (Clough) would give him some friendly banter about that. As time went on, Brian asked me about my general manager:

"How's your mate Brian?"

"Well, he's actually my boss, Brian," I'd reply.

"Does he look after you?"

"Yes, he does," I said. "But he can only do so much. He's a good friend."

I think Brian was keen to know that I was being well looked after at work.

Brian would do whatever he could to help the legion, although he admitted privately to me that he had wished he had done more during a snooker tournament in Derby. He had been asked to appear on television at the event, which was held at the Assembly Rooms. He wanted me to accompany him and shortly after we arrived the former world championship referee Len Ganley walked by and said hello to Brian. When I was introduced to him, I refused to shake his hand. For a moment, there was an awkward silence, which I quickly broke by adding: "I'm not shaking your hand – you'll break my fingers!" I smiled and they both realised what I meant. Len had recently appeared in a television advert in which he picked up a snooker ball, which had been knocked off the table, and crushed it with his gloved hand, to the astonishment of the players and audience. We had a laugh about it and I shook his hand. Thankfully, there were no broken bones. Brian was interviewed at the tournament and spoke about how much he enjoyed snooker. But afterwards he admitted to me that he wished he had mentioned the Royal British Legion because he played snooker there. He knew it would have been invaluable publicity for the organisation. Nevertheless, Brian did more than enough to support the legion over the years and we were always grateful for his help in saving the Darley Abbey branch.

*   *   *

A lot of Brian's generosity was carried out discreetly, with minimum fuss. When he heard that I was planning to take my Mum and Step-Dad on holiday, he put his hand in his pocket, pulled out a few ten-pound notes and said: "While you're away, treat them to a meal on me. Make sure they enjoy themselves." One of the gifts I still treasure is a tie that Brian gave me. Only a few were made and they had a football symbol on them, with his initials, BC. I was very lucky to get one and Brian was really chuffed when we wore them. But not all his generous intentions went without a hitch. He was travelling in the car with myself and Michael when he told us how he had tried to buy a car as a gift someone. "I had a very funny experience yesterday," he told us, before relating the tale in full. As the recipient of the gift lived some miles away, Brian had phoned the Mercedes dealership in that area and explained that he wanted to buy one of their vehicles as a present for someone who lived locally. During the lengthy phone call, Brian described exactly what he was looking for, including the colour (silver) and all the specifications he wanted the car to have. No expense would be spared. Having continued with his detailed description, Brian eventually let the other person speak – only to discover he had been wasting his time. "I'd been talking to the bloody cleaner for twenty minutes!" he said, still laughing as he told the story.

If we were with a group of people and Brian was on official business, I'd always refer to him as Mr Clough. But in private he insisted that I called him Brian. It took me about five years to feel comfortable doing that, because of the amount of respect I had for him. Don't forget, for many years I had admired his teams, watching as a fan from the terraces. So initially it was difficult to get used to being on first-name terms with a footballing hero. Nevertheless, he would tell me off if I called him 'Mr Clough' during those early years, as our friendship developed. He would say to me: "My name's Brian – I've told you, call me Brian!" Although it didn't seem right for me to do that at first, eventually it became natural. I considered it a huge privilege to be able to feel relaxed talking to him, even though he was in such demand. But when he was with other people in his working environment, I respected his position and never said anything unless he invited me into the conversation. I knew he was doing a job and I was careful not to stick my nose in, if he was talking about his work with other people in the football business. Brian told me he thought I was reliable, that I was there when he needed me, the players liked me and I didn't interfere in things that were none of my business. He would sometimes put his arm around you and give you a kiss on the cheek – that was just his way of showing his respect and affection for you. He never forgot his roots and he looked after his family, although he was never one to shout about that.

When it came to his family, Brian was a private man. He once showed me an unusual piece of furniture at his house in the Derbyshire countryside. "That was my Mam's mangle," he told me. The unusual-looking device, originally used to squeeze water out of wet laundry, had been cleaned-up and restored. Brian had then kept it at his house so that it reminded him of his mother and all the efforts she made for the family, including his five brothers and two sisters (another sister died before he was born). Brian was always proud of his family. His Dad, Joseph, became manager at a sweet factory and was a keen football follower. Some of the great Middlesbrough players of the time would go to the factory and Joseph would give them sweets. Meanwhile, Brian's Mum ran the house, making sure everything was clean and tidy and that food was on the table at mealtimes. In Brian's original autobiography he made a point of stressing how grateful he was for the security and peace of mind the whole family gained from her always being there and making their home the best place to be. "She turned that little house into a palace," he said. As a result, his Mum's mangle had pride of place in his own home many years later, a symbol of the values that stemmed from his family.

By complete coincidence, I have now got a similar mangle, which belonged to my late Great Auntie Beattie. She died at the age of ninety and it is incredible to think she had used the mangle right up until her final days. She used to put heavy-duty bedding through it! I decided to keep it as a memory of her and Great Uncle George, who died when he was ninety-one. Brian and Barbara came to George's ninetieth birthday party which was held at the Jubilee Club at Nottingham Forest's City Ground. Auntie Beattie was very forthright but wonderful for her age. She loved Brian and made a real fuss of him. Brian had a laugh and a joke with her and I remember him saying with a smile: "Hey, Auntie Beattie, it's Uncle George's party, not yours – behave yourself!" It was fantastic to see Brian and Barbara sitting there amongst all my family, chatting away and enjoying themselves. During the evening, there were many photographs taken, including one of Brian with me and my brother Trevor. Our relationship wasn't all about football – we were very good, close friends.

As well as holding social events there, the Jubilee Club was always a popular place to meet after matches. Michael and I were among the first members there. Years later, when it developed into a restaurant, the subscription for members went up. The couple that ran it - Ron and Val – gave Michael and I a card each, making us life members. That was in recognition of all the custom we brought in for them – in the form of friends and associates who joined us. But then one of the directors told us we had no right to be life members. Although we argued our case, the cards were taken off us. But we still went along to the club. It remained a great place to meet before and after games. The players would go there after matches and we even met England cricketers there.

*   *   *

I never took Brian's kindness for granted. He always tried to do the best for me and said that he was looking after my bosses by arranging tickets for them to sit in the Directors' Box, so that I would hopefully be treated well in return. "I hope they're looking after you," he would say. But when I was made redundant at the age of fifty-nine, it came as a terrible shock. Brian exclaimed: "That's not what I call looking after you – your business is as bad as football!" I'd not done myself any favours when I was asked in an annual appraisal about my plans for the future. I was faced with that age-old question: "Where do you see yourself over the next few years?" I replied that if I hadn't retired by the time I was sixty, I would feel that I hadn't achieved anything. The company bosses later quoted that back at me – when I was fifty-nine – and said that they would have to let me go. At that point in the conversation, I felt I was fighting for my life. I told them I didn't want to leave. They intimated that I had a lot of friends who would look after me. I'm not sure whether they were referring to Brian and other people at Nottingham Forest, but I replied that I didn't know what they meant. I said I had a wife, a mortgage and only a reduced pension to live on. But there was no choice, I had to leave and it was very upsetting at the time. Being made redundant at the age of fifty-nine decimated my pension. I had paid Annual Voluntary Contributions to boost my pension and the forecast for my retirement at sixty-five was absolutely brilliant. But closing the pension when they did meant that I couldn't add any more and it was wrecked. All I had been working for simply crumbled away, as did all my aspirations for the future. I felt I had done a really good job and deserved to be treated a bit better. I think that was shown less than a year later when I returned to the company, but this time as a contractor. I was my own boss. Brian was delighted for me. "Well done, Col," he said. "They should have looked after you." To this day, I regret telling them that I was aiming to retire at sixty. I suppose I was being bigheaded at the time, but I shouldn't have said it. It gave them an excuse to let me go.

Although I still have regrets about what happened at work, I always got on well with my boss at Pork Farms. When I designed a piece of equipment to make mini pork pies (called Mini Meltons) I took the idea to Brian Stein and he then had a meeting with Marks and Spencer in London. I'm pleased to say M&S took the very first order and the mini pork pies became a huge success. They became so popular that the company wanted to make thousands of them every hour. I was even flown out to see a design team in Holland in order to manufacture them in large quantities. Eventually, some were served on Concorde and I understand they were also served to the Queen at Cheltenham Racecourse – and she enjoyed them! I had modified old machines to make this revolutionary product and nowadays it seems many companies are enjoying success making similar things, with mini versions of all types of food items. But looking back, I wish I had received greater reward and recognition for coming up with this idea. It still leaves a sour taste for me when I reflect on the success of those products.

*   *   *

After all the talk earlier about the Royal British Legion, I can't end this section without mentioning my friend Brian Cullen, who was a Captain in the Royal Scots Dragoon Guards. Brian (Clough) always made him welcome at the City Ground and invited him to watch Forest play several times. When Captain Cullen invited Irene and I over to Germany, where he was stationed, I thought it would be a great idea to take some souvenirs, which could raise some money for the regiment. With this in mind, I approached two major names from the world of football management in Scotland, Jock Stein and Sir Alex Ferguson, when they were among the visitors in the guest room at the City Ground after a match. Both of them agreed to sign a couple of match day programmes, which were raffled off when I took the prized items to Germany. At the time I met the two Scottish managers, the Royal Scots Dragoon Guards had been awarded a gold disc for their version of 'Amazing Grace.' As a result, they had played at a Scotland match at Hampden Park. "I'm sure you were there," I suggested to Jock Stein and Sir Alex, who replied: "Yes – they played better than the teams."

Incidentally, the journey I mentioned to watch Frank Sinatra perform at the Royal Albert Hall was not the only trip organised by Brian for a special event. A group of us, including Brian, went to the horse racing for the day at the Cheltenham Gold Cup in March 1983. Forest's coach driver, Albert, agreed to take us there and back. As you would expect when Brian was involved, we all had VIP tickets. It was a superb day, even though I backed quite a few losing horses. When we returned to the coach, Brian was beaming because he had chosen a winner. It was the fifth race of the day and he had backed a horse called Dish Cloth. With a name like that, it's no wonder Brian cleaned-out the bookies for that race.

11.

The Final Seasons

I feel certain that if Brian had won the FA Cup in 1991, he would have then taken the decision to retire. It would have been the right time for him to take his bow after all he had achieved in football management. And if that had been the case, it would have avoided that terrible final season in which his side was relegated from the Premier League. I think retirement had crossed his mind during the 1990–91 season. The FA Cup Final would have provided the ideal opportunity. Every trophy he won was special to him, whether it be the European Cup, the League Championship trophy, the Simod Cup, the Littlewoods Cup – or the ZDS Cup. He once said that he gained immense satisfaction from winning the Anglo-Scottish Cup with Forest in 1976 because it was his first piece of silverware with the club and it established the right mind-set to be winners.

Yes, all those trophies were satisfying up to a point. But Brian would have loved to have won the FA Cup in 1991, when Forest reached the final. He would have been so proud to hold that trophy on the balcony of the Council House in Nottingham in front of thousands of adoring Forest fans. At that point he could then have stepped back and said to himself: "I've done it." It was also around this time in his career that a group of us were travelling up the M1 on the way to a match – all of us having a good laugh and enjoying each other's company – when Brian turned to me and said: "Col, all of you, just remember this. Enjoy it. Enjoy what we're doing. Enjoy it while you can, it won't be here forever." He didn't say any more, but something was clearly on his mind.

It was also around the time of the 1990–91 season that Brian and I used to talk about what we were going to do when we retired. He would say to me: "Well, Col, you can only go on so many holidays." Knowing how much we both loved cricket, I suggested that one thing we could look forward to was going to watch a Test Match in the West Indies when England played there. I knew that Brian would have the contacts to arrange it and he would enjoy watching that type of match in the company of people such as his good friend Geoff Boycott. "Yes, that would be good, wouldn't it?" Brian would say whenever we discussed the idea, before adding: "I'd love to do something like that with you." But it was really fantasyland for us. It never happened. It all sounded great when we were both working, looking ahead to our retirement. But when retirement finally arrives, your whole outlook changes and the dreams do not always come to fruition.

There is no doubt in my mind that Brian was robbed of the FA Cup in that 1991 Final against Spurs. As with previous Wembley finals, I had travelled down to the twin towers on a coach with Brian's family and friends. When the match started, I was willing Forest to victory, so Brian could have the one trophy he had never won. But the referee had an awful game and failed to punish Paul Gascoigne for two of the most horrendous challenges I have ever seen on a football pitch. If Gazza had been sent-off instead of being stretchered off then I am convinced that Forest would have gone on to lift the cup. But Gascoigne was seen as a national treasure at the time and the referee, Roger Milford, seemed to have stars in his eyes. In my opinion, he failed to do the right thing and show Gascoigne a red card. Gazza was clearly pumped up for the game, but he was fortunate to still be on the pitch after a chest-high challenge on Garry Parker in the opening minutes. He escaped with a lecture from Milford. But he had not learned his lesson. Moments later he lunged wildly at Gary Charles, a terrible challenge which was deserving of a red card itself, never mind what had happened to Parker shortly before. Stuart Pearce scored from the resulting free-kick. Gascoigne had ruptured a cruciate ligament in his right knee and was stretchered from the pitch. But instead of being punished and playing the rest of the game with ten men, Spurs were getting stronger as the game went on. A goal by Paul Stewart brought the two sides level. When the match went into extra-time, it did not surprise me that Brian decided not to join his players on the pitch. That was Brian – he had his own way of doing things. All the media seemed to expect that he would walk on to the famous turf and give his players a very public team-talk. But I suspect that he thought to himself: "They know what they're doing – they don't need me out there. They know what I expect and what I want." And in doing that, he was giving the players huge credit. Unfortunately, extra time went in Spurs' favour and they won 2–1, but I still do not blame Brian for not going on the pitch. It was clearly not going to be Forest's day, whatever he did. When I returned to the City Ground that evening, I met some of the players at the Jubilee Club. Garry Parker lifted up his shirt and showed us the stud marks on his chest. A nice present left behind by Mr Gascoigne. I have read since that he wishes he had been sent off after that initial challenge – it might have spared him all the anguish that followed because he was never the same player again.

It is strange how the FA Cup was the one trophy that eluded Brian during his outstanding career. In the seasons leading-up to that 1991 final, Forest had come very close. Brian's teams had done so well in other competitions that we virtually had season tickets for Wembley. Brian joked that the Forest team coach knew its own way there. But the FA Cup was the one that always got away. Even when the Reds were winning European Cups, the furthest they reached in the competition was the fifth round when they lost 1–0 to Arsenal in front of nearly 36,000 fans at the City Ground in February 1979. The following season they lost in the fourth round at home to Liverpool, despite having beaten them in the League Cup semi-final a few days before. But it was quite understandable, as Forest were chasing honours on several fronts and the matches came thick and fast. By the end of the season in 1980 they had retained the European Cup, won the European Super Cup, were runners-up at Wembley in the League Cup Final and finished fifth in the First Division.

There was added spice to the third round match in 1983 when Forest were drawn away to arch-rivals Derby, who were then managed by Peter Taylor. As far as Brian was concerned, it became a game to forget as the Reds lost 2–0. But there was another early exit from the competition the following year, this time at the hands of Southampton, when a Paul Hart goal was not enough to beat the Saints at home. It was not a major issue though, as Forest finished third in the league and were playing an exciting, attacking style of football, which saw them score more goals than anyone else in the First Division that season. It was the type of football Brian preached about. Forest failed to go beyond the third or fourth rounds for the next few seasons. But all that changed in 1988, when victories over Halifax Town, Leyton Orient, Birmingham City and Arsenal led the Reds to the FA Cup semi-final against Liverpool. The match at Sheffield Wednesday's Hillsborough ground resulted in a close 2–1 defeat, with a goal from Brian's son, Nigel. The following season, hopes were high once again as Forest reached another FA Cup semi-final – against the same opponents and at the same venue. Only this time there were tragic consequences that I, and many others, will never forget.

In a season in which Forest finished third in the league, the Reds had performed well to beat Ipswich Town, Leeds United, Watford and then Manchester United to reach the semi-final in 1989. For the match at Watford, the Reds were in fine form from the kick-off, forcing ten corners in the opening fifteen minutes. Despite the early pressure, it was the home side that almost opened the scoring when a header from Garry Thomson eluded goalkeeper Steve Sutton and was dramatically cleared from the line by Stuart Pearce. The sixth round tie at Old Trafford was the toughest Forest had faced in the competition that season. That game was won with a goal just before half-time. The speedy Franz Carr was impressive down the right and his low cross was side-footed into the net by Garry Parker. It set-up the semi-final against Kenny Dalglish's Liverpool.

The fifteenth of April 1989 had started as a lovely sunny day as we arrived in Sheffield for the game. I remember seeing the Liverpool fans enjoying themselves in the sunshine outside the ground before the match. They had congregated wherever they could to enjoy the atmosphere; it was like a sea of red. And who could blame them? The day of the semi-final was meant to be exciting, something to be enjoyed. Michael (Keeling) and I had approached Hillsborough in the car from the Liverpool-end of the ground. We had driven Brian up the M1 in the car and dropped him off at a hotel near Barnsley so he could meet the Forest team coach there. I was part of the VIP's who enjoyed a special lunch at Hillsborough before the game, not knowing the awful events that were to follow shortly afterwards. I was sitting in the area of the Directors' Box when the game got underway and witnessed at close quarters the tragic events unfold at the Liverpool end of the ground.

I did not realise how serious the problem was at first. I understand that by about ten to three, the two central pens at the Liverpool end (Leppings Lane) were full, but thousands of fans were still waiting outside the ground to get in. A couple of minutes later the Police ordered a large exit gate to be opened to alleviate the crush outside. Around two-thousand support- ers then made their way into the stadium and headed straight for a tunnel leading towards those central pens. That influx of fans inevitably caused severe crushing, with the supporters at the front being pressed against the security fencing. I could see fans climbing over the side fences to try and escape, while others were being lifted by hand, by their fellow supporters, into the upper tier. Within a few minutes of the game kicking-off, it was abandoned. I could see Police officers desperately trying to pull down the fencing to relieve the pressure that had built-up within the pens. I watched helplessly as some Forest fans ran from the other side of the ground to try and help. Supporters were ripping down advertising hoardings to use as makeshift stretchers. There were attempts to revive people at the side of the pitch. I remember an awful, deathly silence as people began to realise the extent of the terrible events in front of them. An ambulance arrived on the pitch, but it was too little too late. The story of the Hillsborough Disaster, in which ninety-six Liverpool fans died, has been well documented over the years. A report by Lord Justice Taylor criticised the Police for their failure to handle the build-up of fans outside the ground properly – and their slow reaction to the disaster as it unfolded.

Some years afterwards, in his first autobiography, Brian made some controversial comments about the events at Hillsborough, which upset a lot of Liverpool fans. But, like many other people, he had been given the wrong information about what happened on that fateful day. In September 2012, the Hillsborough Independent Panel concluded that Police had deliberately altered witness statements in an attempt to blame Liverpool fans for the fatal crush. It also found that crowd safety was 'compromised at every level.' Yet a few years before he died, Brian had already made his feelings clear in a magazine column. He said he had not accused the Liverpool supporters of being thugs, he had actually said the Police made serious errors of judgement. He had been misinformed, but he apologised for any hurt he may have caused and thanked the Liverpool supporters for their kind treatment of his son Nigel, who had left Forest to play for Liverpool when his Dad retired.

On the return journey from Hillsborough on that terrible day, there was little said to each other in the car as we took Brian home, having met the coach at a designated point to pick him up. We were all devastated. The replay, three weeks later at Old Trafford, had a strange atmosphere. I just knew it was not going to be Forest's year. There was huge public sympathy for Liverpool, quite understandably in the circumstances, and therefore it was natural to think it was going to be their year to win the cup. The tragic events at Hillsborough overshadowed the occasion and Forest were not going to win that re-arranged match, however hard they tried. The writing was on the wall within the opening few minutes when Liverpool took the lead with a John Aldridge goal. Although Neil Webb equalised with a lovely shot from outside the penalty area after just over half-an-hour, Aldridge made it 2–1 before an own goal from Brian Laws made it 3–1. And to rub it in, Aldridge ruffled Laws' hair after he had put the ball into his own net. That gesture was completely uncalled for, given the terrible circumstances in which the game was being played. Aldridge's actions were unsportsman-like and I find it very difficult to forgive him for what he did. I understand he has since apologised to Laws, but in my opinion it does not excuse what was a distasteful and unnecessary gesture. Can you imagine what would have happened if a Forest player had done that? As well as having to face the full force of their manager's anger, they would have been roundly cas-tigated by the general public and the media. But, as I have said, the over-whelming public sympathy on the day was with Liverpool, who went on to beat Everton in the final. My sympathies will always remain with the families of all those innocent people who lost their lives after getting into Hillsborough in good time in order to get a good view. Everyone should expect to go to a football match in safety and come away again to tell the tale. The memories of that day, the darkest British football has known, are like a nightmare.

Despite being knocked out of the FA Cup at the semi-final stage, there is no doubt that by 1989 Brian had done a wonderful job in re-building a Forest side which won plaudits far and wide. He had five internationals in the team, namely Stuart Pearce, Des Walker, Steve Hodge, Neil Webb and his own son, Nigel. Only Arsenal and Liverpool won more points than them during the season. Brian's achievements in that 1988–89 season were summed-up brilliantly by a photograph which filled the two centre pages of the match day programme for the team's last game of the season against West Ham. He was pictured alongside the Littlewoods and Simod Cups, holding a cheque for £250 for being the Barclays Manager of the Month for April (a month in which Forest had lifted both trophies and beaten Norwich City, Southampton and Middlesbrough in the league). The title at the top of the photo was: 'Thanks for a great season.' It gave Brian immense satisfaction to have successfully re-built a Forest side, which played the game in the way he insisted it should be played, on the floor with quick neat passing. Yes, it would have been nice to have added the FA Cup to the honours that season, but as Brian said himself: "We'll be back next year."

Unfortunately, Forest's luck in the FA Cup ran out very early in the following season's campaign when they were knocked-out in the third round, in a match which is widely seen as having kept Alex Ferguson in his job at Manchester United. It was 7 January, 1990. Without a victory since mid-November and with United plummeting down the table, there were suggestions that Ferguson might not last much longer at Old Trafford. United's chairman insisted that his manager would not lose his job if they lost at Forest, but defeat would surely not have helped his plight. As it turned out, defeat for United was avoided thanks to young Mark Robins and a header that would be forever labelled 'the goal that saved Fergie's job.' United went on to win the cup that season, beating Crystal Palace in the Final following a replay.

Then came that one season when Brian took his team to the FA Cup Final. They had needed two replays to get past Crystal Palace in the third round. But that only served to fuel the thought that this could be Forest's year. Replays were also needed against Newcastle United and Southampton, but again Forest's resilience suggested that, this time, they could be bound for Wembley. And so it turned out to be, following a superb 4–0 semi-final win over West Ham in the Villa Park sunshine. But the injustice of the Gascoigne controversy in that final against Spurs left a bad taste and the feeling that Brian and the FA Cup were a partnership that was not meant to be. Despite reaching the sixth round the following season and the fifth round in his final season at the City Ground, it remained the one trophy he could not win. They talk about the 'romance of the cup,' but for Brian that particular courtship did not end happily.

In some respects, losing that FA Cup Final was the sign of things to come. I don't think it did Brian any good at all. In the following two seasons, he didn't seem like the manager he had been. I think the pressure was taking its toll. I did my very best to be there for him when he needed me. But I was not involved in any decisions or detailed discussions on footballing matters. I was there as a friend to offer my support when he needed it.

Brian admitted that finishing bottom of the league in that final season devastated him. The 1992–93 season had started so full of promise and excitement. But it ended in bitter disappointment. He spoke to me about his frustration during that fateful season, having enjoyed so many wonderful achievements at Nottingham Forest. I was not involved in any conversations about the announcement of his retirement, and didn't expect to be, so it came as a complete surprise to me when it was officially confirmed that he was standing down from the position he had made his own at the City Ground. As I've said, the season began so full of optimism, as football seasons usually do. The opening match was at home to Liverpool and it was the first Premier League game to be shown live on Sky TV, on 16 August, 1992. Teddy Sheringham scored the only goal of the game to secure the three points for Forest and I remember thinking at the time that we had such a wonderful season ahead of us. It was a marvellous strike by Sheringham, whose shot flew past David James in the visitors' goal after 28 minutes. Scot Gemmill had passed the ball to him and I understand that he initially thought about laying it back into the middle, but when no defender came towards him he simply unleashed a shot, which finished in the top corner.

But the sale of Sheringham to Spurs later that month proved costly for Forest, even though Brian told me he felt he had no choice but to let him go. After the home victory against Liverpool, there were away defeats to Sheffield Wednesday and Oldham Athletic. The game against Oldham proved to be Sheringham's last in a Forest shirt. He had been a great signing for Forest, joining from Millwall in July 1991 for two million pounds and becoming the leading scorer in his one and only full season with Forest. Brian did not want Sheringham to leave, but the striker told him he wanted to be near his young son, which was understandable. We were having lunch at a hotel on the M62 (I think it was before the game against Oldham) when Brian asked his coach, Liam O'Kane, to fetch Sheringham so he could have a word with him.

"Now then son," said Brian. "Has the situation changed with you and your bairn?"

"No, boss," replied Sheringham.

"So you want to go back down south, then?"

"That's right boss."

At that point, Brian confirmed a deal would be agreed. Sheringham went on to sign for Spurs. Brian knew there was no point in keeping a player who did not want to be at the club and needed to be near his son. But I think Brian was left feeling even more disappointed when the striker left Spurs a few years later and moved to Manchester United. It appeared that the issue of living in the south of England to be near his son was no longer an issue. The problem for Brian, and the club, was that Sheringham was never adequately replaced. It signalled a worrying slide in Forest's fortunes. Gary Bannister and Robert Rosario were brought in to wear the Number 10 shirt during the season, but it was not enough. The sale of Des Walker to the Italian club Sampdoria was also beginning to have an effect in defence.

Despite two goals from Bannister in the match at Oldham, Forest lost 5–3. Brian said Forest had been "well and truly whacked." A string of six consecutive defeats included losses to Manchester United, Norwich, Blackburn and Sheffield Wednesday. In the 2–1 defeat to Wednesday, Bannister scored his fourth goal in five games, heading past Forest's former goalkeeper Chris Woods. But the Reds had already been trailing 2–0 and the solitary goal was just a consolation. There had been moments when the fans thought Forest might have got something from the game, such as when a typically thunderous free-kick from Stuart Pearce clipped the foot of the post. But it summed-up the Reds' luck at that time.

Forest played some wonderful football during Brian's final season. But they had some atrocious luck too. I came away from many matches wondering how Brian's team had actually lost. The run of defeats was eventually brought to a halt in a Monday night match against Coventry City, which was televised live (perhaps Sky TV was bringing them good luck?). Before the game, Brian thanked the fans for their patience and support and said he would do his best to repay them. The Reds stopped the rot with 1–1 draw against City, thanks to a goal from Brian's son, Nigel. He earned his side a point with an equaliser in the second half, after Robert Rosario had put the visitors ahead on the stroke of half-time (before he joined the Reds later in the season). But after eight games, Forest were bottom of the league – a position they unfortunately became used to that season. Some relief was provided by a competition which had generated success for Brian in the past – the League Cup, or Coca Cola Cup as it was known then. In their second round first-leg match at Stockport County, Forest enjoyed a 3–2 win over the club two divisions below them (Stockport were in the new Second Division). Brian was impressed with how Stockport played and commented on their six-foot seven-inch striker Kevin Francis, who had signed from Derby County and scored both goals for the home side. Brian joked that he was tall enough to clean his upstairs window without a ladder! Des Walker was in the crowd to watch his former teammates win 2–1 in the second leg. Kingsley Black had given Forest the lead on the night, while a Pearce free-kick was deflected into the goal by County defender Jim Gannon.

The visit of Brian's former side Middlesbrough was a highlight in those early months of the season – because it gave Forest their second league victory. Kingsley Black scored the only goal of the game. Brian was pleased to see his home town club back in the top flight of football, but he was even more delighted to get three points in that mid-week fixture. He was desperate to give Forest fans something to smile about and he insisted that his side should stick to his passing style of play. In the previous game, Arsenal came to the City Ground and won 1–0, despite the Reds coming close to at least a draw. A shot by Gary Crosby beat the Gunners' 'keeper, David Seaman, but struck the inside of the post and rolled along the line without actually going in. It was yet another sign of Forest's bad luck in that frustrating season. I remember one afternoon, around the time results were not going too well, we stopped the car on the way home so he could get out and stretch his legs. He still felt the pain from his injured knee and it was good for him to have a little walk after sitting in the car for a long time. As we walked along together, he leaned on me a little and we talked about how things were going. He was clearly frustrated but he wanted to do all he could to get Forest out of the mess they were in.

Before the final game of October, against Ipswich at home, the Reds were still bottom of the league, but only a point from getting out of the relegation zone. Yet hopes of escaping from the bottom three were dashed when Ipswich won 1–0. Everton won by the same score-line the following week and the gap to safety had extended to four points before the final match of November, which saw Southampton leave the City Ground with a 2–1 victory, despite Brian welcoming back Neil Webb. He had re-joined the club from Manchester United and was frustrated to see a goal attempt ruled out for offside. The points gap following that game became five points, which meant at least two wins were needed – but league victories were still hard to achieve.

Once again, the League Cup provided some much needed relief, when Forest beat Spurs 2–0 at the start of December. Thankfully, that momentum was continued into the next league game at Elland Road, with two goals from Roy Keane helping the Reds beat champions Leeds United 4–1. That win earned Forest the award of 'Barclays Performance of the Week.' It was all the more impressive considering that the result was Leeds' first home defeat in 32 league games. But Brian was frustrated when his side played well in the following match, at Aston Villa, yet came away with nothing. It was a storyline that was becoming worryingly familiar. Hopes were raised for a Forest win at home to Wimbledon after Nigel scored in the opening five minutes. It ended in a 1–1 draw.

The final match of 1992 was a 2–1 defeat at Spurs, but the New Year started brightly with a win in the FA Cup third round over Southampton and league victories over Coventry away and Chelsea at home. Gary Bannister scored twice in the 3–0 win against Chelsea, heading home an Ian Woan free-kick for his second. The Icelandic international Toddi Orlygsson got the third, late in the game. Further victories against Oldham and Middlesbrough, along with a goalless draw at Anfield, helped to lift Forest to the position of third from bottom, just two points from safety and with two games in hand. Although they edged out of the relegation zone with five wins in seven games, they were third from bottom at the start of April, with just eight games to go. Before a home match against Aston Villa, the Reds were only a point from safety. But by then they had lost the captain, Stuart Pearce, because of a groin injury, which required an operation. There is no doubt that the Reds missed Pearce's influence in the final few months of the season. Brian admitted that to me as we travelled in the car one day. I was driving and Brian was in the passenger seat, with his feet perched up on the dashboard. He described how frustrated he was that the team was missing the presence of the captain. There were also problems over a new contract for Pearce, which made matters even more difficult. We talked things over as we continued the journey in the car and, at one point in the conversation, I even suggested to Brian that he could think about selling Pearce if things were that bad. But he said it was something he could not begin to contemplate at that stage and he said he would 'sleep on it.' I think this showed how much credit Brian gave Pearce. Not only was he a fantastic player but he was a superb motivator too. I regarded him as one of the main components of the Forest engine – and without him it was very difficult to get anywhere when the team faced an uphill task.

On Brian's 58th birthday, his relatives from Middlebrough – regular visitors to the City Ground – came to watch the game at home to Leeds United, and brought him a birthday cake. The match saw Nigel switch from centre-forward to defence, playing alongside Carl Tiler. Although Leeds' Rod Wallace gave the champions an early 1–0 lead, Brian's son stepped-up to slot home a 25th minute penalty in front of the Bridgford End, sending Leeds 'keeper John Lukic the wrong way. Forest won the spot kick after Ian Woan had gone down in a challenge with Lukic. The visitors hung-on for a 1–1 draw and although the penalty would have given Brian something to smile about on his birthday, he said he would have preferred to celebrate with three points. That result lifted Forest off the foot of the Premier League for 24 hours. Although Nigel scored again in the next match against Southampton, with a Roy Keane goal also helping them to a 2–1 win, there were defeats to Aston Villa, Blackburn Rovers and Queens Park Rangers. In a television interview after a match, Ray Stubbs bravely asked the question: "How can you be bottom of the Premier League?"

Brian replied: "Well, to be fair, it's kept me awake four or five nights every week in the last three months and I don't know how we're bottom of the Premier League, but we are bottom and you've got to be realistic. Until we get away from the bottom, people like you, Raymond, will keep asking me these questions." His voice then rose steadily until it reached a crescendo with the final sentence. "We've got to get away from the bottom of that league. I am sick of being bottom of that league."

But Forest were beginning to run out of games to save themselves and, despite a 2–1 win against Spurs in the penultimate home match of the season, relegation was confirmed when the Reds lost 2–0 to Sheffield United at the City Ground. By then, Brian's retirement had been officially announced, albeit prematurely by the club chairman. It meant that, although Forest were relegated, there was still a huge amount of respect and warmth shown to him by supporters of both sides at that final home game. Unfortunately, it was a match I actually missed – because I was on holiday. I had booked the break some months before, not expecting that particular Saturday would be so significant. To this day, I still hope it didn't appear that I was deliberately away for such a momentous match. It was simply something I had not envisaged when I booked the holiday. I met Brian many times afterwards and he certainly did not hold it against me. He probably wished he had been on holiday too and that the whole end to that season had been a horrible dream. It is definitely not the way he should be remembered, after all the success he had brought to the club and the city of Nottingham. Just a few weeks before his retirement, he had been given the Freedom of Nottingham in recognition of his remarkable achievements. He became the first recipient of the accolade since the Olympic champion ice dancers Jayne Torvill and Christopher Dean ten years before. Forest finished the season bottom of the league, nine points from safety, and saying goodbye to the man who had brought them success beyond my, and everyone's, wildest dreams. Thankfully, I was in the fortunate position of not having to say goodbye – and kept in touch with Brian during his retirement.

12.

Farewell My Friend

I kept my season tickets at Forest after Brian retired and continued to watch the Reds – it was my small way of keeping his memory alive at the City Ground. The chairman and other people at the club knew I still had contact with Brian and they would ask me how he was. I wanted to make sure that he was not forgotten, even though a new era was underway. Brian stayed away from the City Ground for a few years but I still had access to the guest room where I could meet friends. The words of the former chairman Maurice Roworth often came to mind: that I would always be welcomed as a friend of the club. It was in the guest room that I met Roy Keane again when he returned as a Manchester United player. I'm pleased to say he remembered me and I introduced him to a friend of mine from Alfreton who had just picked-up an injury while playing Sunday league football. Roy was absolutely charming and my friend was on cloud nine when Roy gave him some advice on how to deal with the injury. I also met the former Notts County manager Jimmy Sirrell and had a chat with him. But talking to Jimmy was a bit like chatting to Bill Shankly – the footballing technical terms they both used were like jargon to me. It went way over my head. I mentioned to Jimmy that I was still in touch with Willie Carlin. "How is the wee lad?" said Jimmy. "Is he OK?" He said he would like to meet Willie again because he was one of his former players. So I arranged for them to meet and have a meal together at the Italian restaurant on Trent Bridge. I then took them to a game and into the guest room afterwards. They were both talking to a few former players they had known, including Graeme Souness. It was a lovely little re-union and Willie later repaid the compliment by inviting me into the guest room at Derby County. While I was there I had a good chat with Dave Mackay and we later came back to Nottingham together on the train. But the world of football was not the same without Brian.

As time went by, I would visit Brian every four to six weeks. On one of the visits I drove him out to Ashover in Derbyshire with his former assistant Ron Fenton. We stopped at a little place, which had wonderful views of the countryside. I told them it served fantastic fish and chips. We sat in a little annex and the waiter brought us the food. When he saw Brian, he stopped in his tracks and said: "Don't I know you?" Brian replied: "You might do, Sir, but I don't know you." That comment broke the ice and we had a laugh about it. I drove Brian back through some scenery I thought he would like and when we reached his home he thanked me for a lovely day. Ron Fenton asked me to join him at a match at Stoke City, where Forest were playing. Ron was scouting for England at the time and we went into the guest room and met all the Forest representatives. It was good to see them. Ron invited me to several other matches and told me he had been looking at Steve Stone, who went on to win a few caps for England. On another occasion, a group of us, including Brian, Barbara and my wife Irene, went to Newstead Abbey in Nottinghamshire – the ancestral home of Lord Byron. We met in the village of Linby and when we arrived at the abbey Brian was in his element. He loved the gardens there. Afterwards, we all went to a pub in Linby, where the landlord and landlady were overwhelmed to see Brian. They provided us with some lovely food and it turned out to be a very relaxing and enjoyable afternoon.

In September 1999, Brian made an emotional return to the City Ground and received a hero's welcome. It was a celebration of the renaming of the Executive Stand, which he had been instrumental in having built in the first place. It now bears his name. He also unveiled a bust and at half-time strode on to the pitch to acknowledge the applause and cheers from fans.

"I'm delighted to be back," he said. "I've had to find my bearings because it's been a long time since I was last here but the reception could not have been much better. They've changed a few things – such as the chairman – but it's a lovely feeling." As he held court with the media, the subject of two European Cups and a league championship was mentioned and a question raised about whether it could ever be achieved again. "It will be difficult but the opportunity is there," he said. "That's why our football is so good. We did it rather quickly, in fact, not many people noticed, and what really gets up my nose is hearing about Manchester United. Alex (Ferguson) is an excellent manager but he used to come here when United were languishing in the First Division as it then was. How long did it take them to win the championship and the European Cup?"

A few years later, in May 2003, Brian was given the Freedom of Derby – to accompany the Freedom of Nottingham he had received ten years before. He visited the old Baseball Ground and told reporters: "It brings back beautiful memories." A vintage Rolls Royce picked him up from his home and took him on a tour of some of his favourite places. They included Darley Park, where he used to take his sons to play football. He also planted a tree on the banks of the River Derwent. At Derby County's Pride Park Stadium he was presented with the freedom scroll. The Mayor, Robin Turner, described Brian as a, "rare individual and a unique talent who brought honour to our football club and reflected glory to the city." In response, Brian said: "It's a tremendous honour. Having come to Derby 35 years ago ... you couldn't get rid of me. We have been extremely happy here."

Brian had also appeared as a special guest at a football forum at Pride Park, hosted by the radio station Century FM, and was again in fine form as he answered questions from the audience. Referring to Alex Ferguson and the number of European Cups both men had won, the Master Manager commented: "For all his horses, knighthoods and championships, he hasn't got two of what I've got. And I don't mean balls!" There was also strong criticism of the FA officials who failed to appoint him as England manager. "I got the feeling that Lancaster Gate were frightened of me," he said. "As interviews go, I felt I had walked it. I had the experience required. But I didn't get it. They appointed Ron Greenwood and he wasn't even on the shortlist!" Raising his voice, he continued: "Ron Greenwood fitted the bill. Their bill. They weren't worried about the standing of English football in Europe. They weren't worried about gates. They were worried about themselves. They didn't want me invading and making waves. I should have had it. The timing was right." There were light-hearted moments too. He burst into song, giving a short rendition of *'You've either got or you haven't got style.'* He then remarked: "And we've got it, haven't we?" Cue lots of applause.

Even in retirement, Brian was still a natural entertainer and was always superb when he stood-up to speak at events and dinners. He made regular appearances on a local radio phone-in and I would pick him up from his home and drive him to the studio and back. On the way, we would have a really interesting conversation in the car about various issues and it would get him 'warmed-up' for his special appearance. His former striker, Garry Birtles, would be a guest with him, but Brian was the undoubted star of the show – and I don't think Garry would mind me saying that. I would often sit with them in the studio and keep as quiet as I could. People across the East Midlands loved to phone-up and speak to their football hero. I also drove Brian to television interviews and he would insist that I sat in the studio. He made sure I was still a part of it all, as his friend. On one occasion the former football manager Ron Atkinson was chatting to Brian. When Ron saw me he said to Brian: "What about your driver?" Brian replied: "He's not my driver. That's Col, he's my mate." A chair was quickly arranged for me and I sat out of camera shot.

I knew he was ill and I visited him in hospital a number of times but I did not realise how serious things were. After he underwent a liver transplant in Newcastle, I visited him at home, but he did not discuss the operation with me. He would ask me about certain people and whether I had seen them. In his final years, I did not get the chance to see him as often as I would have liked. I was struggling with my own health and I could not drive, so it was difficult for me to visit him. During one of my visits to his house, he seemed a bit down in dumps. But then his mood picked-up and he said: "I've got something for you, Col." He gave me a lovely picture of Frank Sinatra. It reminded me of some of the marvellous times we had enjoyed, especially when Brian had arranged that trip to see Old Blue Eyes at the Royal Albert Hall. At first I said I could not accept the picture, as I am sure it meant a lot to him. But he and Barbara agreed I should have it and it remains a special possession.

The last time I saw him was at his house in Darley Abbey, a little village on the outskirts of Derby. He was lying on the settee. As we were chatting, he brought up the subject of a possible knighthood. A campaign had been started by fans who hoped he would be given the honour.

"I'm certain it will get tremendous support," I told him.

Brian was clearly very flattered by all the talk of a possible knighthood and – above all – I think he would have seen it as something special for Barbara, in recognition of all the support she had given him over the years. For those people who may have doubted whether he would have accepted a knighthood, it's clear to me he most certainly would have welcomed it. It is just a shame that despite the public campaign for him to be knighted, it never actually happened. A petition with more than 7,000 signatures was collected while he was still alive. But he died before it could be presented to the government. The petition was handed-in to 10 Downing Street but the government said it could not give a knighthood posthumously, unless it was for someone in the military. Nevertheless, I think the most important thing is that he was aware of the campaign while he was still alive and he knew how much his fans thought of him.

When I heard the news that Brian had died, I was absolutely devastated. To think I had seen him only a few weeks before – it was difficult to take it all in. Like many other people, I had not realised just how ill he was. It came as such a shock. Barbara phoned me to invite me to the memorial service at Derby's Pride Park stadium. The huge turnout that night showed how much people cared for him. It was quite an emotional evening and the weather was awful, with heavy rain and thunder. As Barbara commented, it was probably Brian's way of saying he did not want any fuss. The fact that the service was held in a football stadium made it even more fitting. Among the tributes was one by his friend Geoff Boycott who recalled how Brian had gone to watch him play at Chesterfield. The England batsman was disappointed when he got himself out and was so upset that he stayed in the dressing room. Brian came in to see him and told him: "I know you are down but look at your team-mates outside. They are not sure if they will ever make runs." Brian told Boycott that he would make runs, if not that day, then tomorrow. And if not tomorrow, then the day after. "You've got talent, young man," said Brian. That made the famous cricketer feel ten feet tall, even though he had failed on that particular day. It demonstrated Brian's great ability for man-management.

Martin O'Neill paid a wonderful tribute when he said: "Brian Clough touched the lives of all of us inside this stadium to one extent or another and we'll never forget him. As a player I was terrified of him most of the time, but I'll tell you something, he was a man who, when you felt you couldn't run anymore and that your heart was about to burst, you put in your last ounce of endeavour for." Father Frank Daly, who conducted Brian's funeral, said everyone knew the outspoken side of Brian. "What not many people know are the things he did quietly in so many acts of kindness for very ordinary people, those ordinary people who will miss him because they felt he was their friend," he said.

As I sat there in the stand, listening to the tributes, all the memories came flooding back. I recalled the times that I had called him 'Mr Clough' when we first met and how difficult it had been to refer to him as 'Brian' even though he insisted. It seemed to take me ages to call him by his first name, simply because of the respect I had for him. But he would tell me off if I used the wrong name. He would say: "My name's Brian. I've told you before, call me Brian." Eventually, I felt comfortable using his first name and it felt like the most natural thing in the world. I thought about the times we enjoyed going to Wembley – and how I had managed to secure some FA Cup Final tickets for him in later years, thanks to a friend of mine who had connections with the FA. Looking back it seemed very fitting that I should obtain Cup Final tickets for him. 'After all, among my first questions to Brian, as a fan all those years ago had been whether he could do the same for me.

After Brian had passed away, there were times when I joined his family in going to see Burton Albion play and I enjoyed watching Nigel in charge of the team there. I offered to buy a season ticket at Burton but Nigel, who shares his Dad's generous nature, said I didn't need to buy one. Before the games, Elizabeth would pick me up from the railway station and we would go Burton's Eton Park ground. I would also meet Percy Simmons who was a mutual friend. After the match, we would all go back to Barbara's house and then Elizabeth would take us back to the railway station. They were very enjoyable days out and it was lovely to spend time with Brian's family. Unfortunately, as my health began to fail, those occasions became fewer because I couldn't get out and about as much. In recent years my health has not allowed me to do as much as I would like, but I have managed to return to the City Ground to watch a couple of matches from the comfort of the executive boxes – in the stand named after my mate, the stand he created. As soon as I walked through the door, I felt I had come home. For the first of those games, I was extremely grateful to be invited as a guest of my former secretary, Lesley Roome, who had won a competition. And for the second game, in November 2013, I was there as an official for the Royal British Legion. Forest had donated the executive box for those taking part in the Remembrance Day ceremony on the pitch and I felt proud to host a number of special guests from the Armed Forces and local authority. On each occasion it was wonderful to see all the photographs from the European glory days. It brought back some lovely memories and, just for a short time, I felt I was back in it again.

I have also been back to Cala Millor. But it was not the same without Brian there. Everywhere I went, I expected to see him. Instinctively, I was still looking for him. But instead there was just a huge emptiness. There were some places there that I could not even bring myself to visit because the memories of Brian were so strong. It made me feel too emotional. We had enjoyed so many happy times there. That last visit to Cala Millor made me realise what it was all about: it was the company we shared that was the most important thing. We could have been anywhere – Mablethorpe or Skegness – with respect to those places, but it did not matter. It was who we were with that really made it enjoyable. When there was a group of us together, we had created such a fantastic atmosphere. But that special place in the sunshine no longer seemed so special as I looked around. It was now only special for the memories it held. Back home, I still miss the regular match day experience and the wonderful opportunities that came my way, thanks to Brian. In a strange way, I can understand how players feel when their careers come to an end. The top players usually get the best of everything while they're playing: the best hotels, cars and food, along with all the fame and fortune. Some may not appreciate it until it comes to an end.

Most of all I miss Brian's friendship. I recalled a conversation we once had when he told me how much he appreciated the fact I could be relied upon. He paid me the greatest compliment when he turned to me and said: "If I could have picked another brother, it would have been you."

Brian had some wonderful brothers, so to be even mentioned in their company was a great privilege for me. My valued friendship with Brian led me to enjoy the kind of football experiences I could only have dreamed about as an ordinary fan. To me, it was like fantasy football – but in real life. Yes, I was an ordinary fan who met an extraordinary man. And for that I'll always be grateful. Thanks for the memories Brian, I still miss you.

Printed in Great Britain
by Amazon